I0437352

Player's Anthem

by

Equise J. Smith

authorHOUSE®

AuthorHouse™
1663 Liberty Drive, Suite 200
Bloomington, IN 47403
www.authorhouse.com
Phone: 1-800-839-8640

This book is a work of fiction. People, places, events, and situations are the product of the author's imagination. Any resemblance to actual persons, living or dead, or historical events, is purely coincidental.

© 2007 Equise J. Smith. All rights reserved.

No part of this book may be reproduced, stored in a retrieval system, or transmitted by any means without the written permission of the author.

First published by AuthorHouse   12/3/2007

ISBN: 978-1-4259-9451-8 (sc)

Library of Congress Control Number: 2007900676

Printed in the United States of America
Bloomington, Indiana

This book is printed on acid-free paper.

"Don 't let dreams remain a dream"

A special thanks. . .

I would like to thank my family and friends.

Table of Contents

THE CHARACTER'S BIO

I'm *John Speaks*, "loved by none, hated by all." I'm the type of nigga who gives it to you straight. See, Dave likes to play games, wine an' dine a bitch, whereas I come out and say what's on my fucking mind. If I just wanna fuck, I just wanna fuck. Some bitches catch an attitude; some are down. I don't give a shit. I'm not the relationship-type guy. To sum things up, my motto is "Fuck 'em² before they fuck you."

John Speaks is a twenty-four-year old, six-foot-one-inch, light-skinned brother with braids, hundred-and-eighty-pound and an attitude. Females come to him; he doesn't sweat them. He usually pulls them in with his light-brown eyes, but once he opens his foul mouth, they want no part of him. He barely graduated high school. All he does is try and get by in life. He still lives at home with his dad, who is a womanizer. His mom left them both after she caught his dad cheating numerous times. He never kept a job or girl longer than three months because of his temper. The only person he truly has love for is his friend Pam, but she has never seen him as more than a friend. Plus, she's in love with Dave. John and Dave have always been competitive since kindergarten, fighting over whose the best in everything, but John's no match. Deep down inside he's jealous of Dave. He lives for now, which is pussy and getting high, and fuck anybody who has a problem with that.

I'm *James Andrews*. Truth be told I'm an undercover player. The only true player is Dave. Don't get me wrong, I have skills, but I prefer to do my shit on the lo'. I don't need recognition to boast my ego. I became friends with Dave and John back in my six grade year when I transfer from South side elementary to North side elementary, so you know I ran into some drama. My second day there, three kids were gonna jump me in the bathroom. Dave and John walked in, so I really thought I was gonna get my ass kick. John wanted to help them kick my ass, since some kids from south side jumped him, but Dave told them to leave me alone. He had clout so they step off. I didn't know why he help me then, but I found out later that he had seen me in the mall one day with my sister who he was trying to get wit, so he figure he could use me to get to her. But we ended up becoming real cool friends, so he back off, well that's what he told me. I'm a delivery driver for an auto parts company. It's just something for now until I find my niche. My philosophy on life is "Bragging creates haters, who in turn bring drama." So I let the others get the glory and put my two cents in every now or then.

James Andrews is twenty-five years old. He's five-foot-nine, stocky, bald-headed, brown-skinned with a mustache and a goatee. James likes to play the background. John thinks he rides Dave's jock, but he's just as knowledgeable. He doesn't do his thing in front of others. He'll play along, but for the most part he doesn't like anyone having dirt on him. He always says to the fellas "Can't anybody hold me. I do my dirt all by my lonely."

How u doin'? My name is *Dave Anderson.* I'm twenty-three years old, six-foot-three, cut for a slim guy, a low-haircut dark-skinned man. As far back as I can remember the ladies always flocked to me. Over time I learned the playa game from hanging out with my Dad and watching him work his magic. He used to lie to me and say they were just friends, but I knew what was up. That's why I know what to say and how to get these females to do what I want. I figure women know we're full of shit, but as long as we tell them what they want to hear, they don't care.

Dave Anderson is a guy who was taught early the rules to the game. He never lets his guard down and always wants to control the situation. He doesn't feel he's disrespecting women. He's just doing and giving them what they want. He's so smooth that when he breaks up with them, they don't realize they were played and figured they did something wrong. He knows John is jealous of him, but doesn't sweat it. James is doing his dirt on the lo' and Eric idolizes him. He believes in doing his thing until he can't do it no more.

Hi. I'm *Eric Anderson*, Dave's little brother, I am eighteen, skinny with a baby-fro, brown-skinned with some pimples here and there. I'll admit I'm slow when it comes to women and street life. That's why I hang around my brothers and his friends every chance I get. I'll try to take the good and throw out the bad, which is mostly coming out of John's mouth. I don't want to use women or disrespect them. I just want to be able to talk to them without being nervous. I'm smart and have a bright future, I just graduated high school and plan on going to St. Joseph University, I'm not what women are looking for. Really I don't know what they want. So for now I live my life through my brother and his friends.

Eric is a shy, awkward kind of fellow. Women see from a mile away that he's weak and doesn't have confidence in himself, which turns some of them off. He's not ugly; he just has to learn to stand up straight and be strong and forceful when he talks. He knows he would treat a woman right once he finds one that is interested in him, but if the wrong woman gets her claws in him, he'll get played.

Introduction...................

Every Friday night the fellas gather in the basement of Dave and Eric parent's house, where Dave's room is located. You wouldn't think it was a basement by the way he hooked it up. As you walk down the wooden stairs, there are pictures on the wall of black men dressed as pimps. At the bottom of the steps you are met by black carpet which stretches across the entire basement floor. To the left, lined up against the wall is a black bar and stool set, which is really his dad's. Hanging above it, is that poster every kid father from the seventies had of the different sex position for each zodiac sign. Mounted on the walls in the top corner are small speakers and under them sitting on black round end tables are purple triangle neon lights. As your eyes drift around the room, you come to a brown closet door where taped to it is a poster of Pam Grier from the movie Foxy Brown. The king size bed he sleeps on sits in the middle of the room. On each side, at the top of the bed are two black dressers. And on the wall behind the bed is full length mirror, so he can watch himself in action. A few feet from one of the dressers is a black leather recliner which is facing a Sony 42" inch television, that his dad brought for him as a graduation gift. Next to the recliner is a black leather sofa with a brown hardwood coffee table in front of it. On the other side along the wall is a refrigerator. A few feet in front of that is a cheap kitchen table and chair set. Located on a counter top which he built back in high school as a shop project, is a microwave, toaster and coffee maker. In front of the bed is the stereo system, and next to it is the video game center, that he and his brother play. Then there's another door that leads to the laundry room. Plus his own personal back door entrance, all the way to the left.

When the fellas get together they usually drank, smoke and talk about one thing. Women! How many phone numbers they got that week, what pick up line they used, how long it took for them to get the panties and how they played them afterwards. Everyone usually has a story to tell, except for Eric, who's not really part of the crew.

THE DATING GAME RULES

1. Don't spend your cash and get no ass.

2. If you can get away with a cheap date, then go for it.

3. Never double-date on the first date; if your man is outshining you, you're in trouble.

4. If you think you can hit it on the first date, you probably can. (Alcohol helps)

5. Go for a kiss at the end of the date no matter what. What's the worst that can happen?

6. If she offers to go dutch, let her, but that means no ass.

7. If you're not a talker, go see a movie.

8. If you're trying to impress her, be creative.

9. Dress up nice on the first date.

10. Remember on the first date you're sending your representative; It's not the real her or you.

CHAPTER I
Pussy Makes The World Go Round

Look man, I don't understand women, and I'm gonna stop trying, said a frustrated Eric, sitting on the edge of his brother's Dave bed.

You mean all this time yo ass been tryin' to figure them out? James question, taking a puff of a blunt he just rolled leaning back in the recliner. Yous' a dumb ass.

Whateva! Responded Eric flagging him with his right hand.

E, pay attention. I'm gonna tell you the three hardest things in life, said his brother Dave. Laying back in his bed with his slim six-foot-three frame, dark-skinned complexion and his fresh fade hair cut. Dress in his work attire, dress shirt and slacks, that he wears selling cars at his uncles car lot. Fellas, correct me if I'm wrong. Number one, holding up his right arm and hand with one finger extended up to the ceiling getting their attention. Pulling out when the volcano is about to erupt.

"Tru Dat" affirmed James. Who's twenty-five years of age, five-foot nine, stocky and bald, brown skin complexion with a mustache and goatee.

Number two, raising another finger. Reaching for a hat when your about to get in that pussy.

Preach on, John endorsed. A twenty-four year old, six-foot- one inch, light-skinned brother with braids, light brown eyes, weighing a hundred-and- eighty pounds with a serious attitude problem.

And number three is trying to understand women.

Soon as he completed his sentence the three of them burst out in laughter knowing they all experienced those situations in the past.

Once the laughter settled down, John decided to add some more information to the conversation as he lays across the couch in his black dickie set with his shirt button from top to bottom and timberland boots to match, drinking a forty. Look! You know my philosophy on life "Fuck'em before they fuck u". If we understood bitches there wouldn't be any problems in this fucked-up world. We men are a simple species. All we want is to make money, eat, get pussy, and get our dicks sucked.

But women, they want it all. Our loot, a house, car, kids, and for you to treat them like a queen while they treat you like shit.

What? Eric blurted out with a perplex look on his face.

Yo Dave! What the fuck is wrong with yo brother? You were supposed to have taught his ass the "Players Anthem."

What's the "Players Anthem"? Eric asked with curiosity.

Well E, said Dave clearing his throat, I guess it's time to school you.

Here, hit this, said James, passing Eric what's left of the blunt he rolled. A few puffs of that shit an' this knowledge we're about to drop will seem real clear to you.

I don't smoke that stuff, looking at it with a look of disgust.

Just smoke the shit and stop acting like a pussy, John demanded.

Eric examines it closely and then slowly puts the bud end to his lips and inhales. Inexperienced with smoking, he begins coughing uncontrollably while the others watch on in laughter.

Having seen enough, John snatches it from him, "Give me that before you kill yourself."

Listen up E, announced Dave getting their attention. Lesson one! Everything a man does in life is for a women.

John and James nod their heads in approval.

You know that saying "Money makes the world go round"? Well fuck that! Fellas, tell'em what makes the world go round.

"Pussy," they shouted.

Pussy? Repeated Eric with a bewilder look.

Yeah, pussy stated Dave. It controls every decision you make. The clothes you buy, the car you drive and the money you make. You need a job for what?

To survive, answered Eric.

Naw nigga, interrupted John. You need a job so you can buy that shit to impress the bitches.

Right, said Dave, affirming John's statement. If you wasn't trying to please the ladies, you wouldn't need all that shit. You could care less about how you look or what you drive. Your ass probably wouldn't even wash up.

But you need money for all that, replied Eric.

You wouldn't need money if it wasn't for the hoes, affirmed John.

Maybe, contemplated Eric, still trying to understand their logic. But that's one thing.

One thing, yelled John.

All right, listen fool, said James.

You want a car?

Yeah, answered Eric.

For what?

To get around.

And what else? Don't front!

Cause girls go for guys with a nice ride, he responded reluctantly.

Right! So when you pull up to a honey in yo whip and she's all on your dick, what's your   next move?

I don't know, said a baffled Eric. I guess getting to know her and making her my girl.

"What?" They all shouted in unison, appalled at his answer.

You don't want to make her your girl, spited James.

Why not? Wondering why they're getting all bent out of shape.

Cause she's probably a chicken head and the only reason she likes you is because of your whip. You just want to set things up so you can tap that ass.

I don't want to use women like that.

Why not? They use us.

I watch my brother and see how much running around and lying he does. This girl, that girl, spending money here and there. I don't want that stress.

Stress, snapped Dave. It's all in good fun.

Spending money, snickered John. You told us you never have to spend money, they're always paying for shit.

They do, but every now and then you have to switch the game up to keep them around.

After you hit that shit, fuck keeping them around, replied John. You know how I do, if I just wanna fuck, I just wanna fuck. Fuck how they feel. Some bitches catch attitude, some are down. I don't give a shit.

Cause if the shit was all that, you never know when you might want to tap it again, responded Dave.

I heard that, agreed James.

Get off his dick. You always riding his dick. I think his ass is being whipped off that chicken head pussy, declared John.

Yo, like my man said in that movie "You don't let the pussy whip you, you whip that pussy" Dave quoted.

Your ass is slippin'. I don't wine an' dine a bitch. I give it to em' straight. I'm not the relationship type nigga.

Fuck you bitch, you handle things your way and I'll handle things mine.

And I'm not on his dick, interrupted James.

Nigga please! You been on his dick since he save your ass back in six grade.

You still on that shit?

Back when they were young, James family move across town. So he had to transfer from South Side Elementary to their rival school North Side Elementary in the middle of his sixth grade year. His second day there, three students were gonna jump him in the bathroom. Dave and John walked in a few minutes afterwards, so he really thought he was gonna get his ass kick. John wanted to help beat him up, since some people from south side jump him. But Dave step in and told them to leave him alone. He was real popular. A lot of people were scared of him and John, who everyone thought was crazy. He only help James cause he knew his sister, who he like. So he figure he could use him. But it back fire, and all three of them became good friends.

Hello, interrupted Eric waving his left hand in the air. I thought we were trying to help me.

Yeah, your right! Y'all chill and let's get back to what we were talking about, said James trying to defuse the tension. What were we talking about?

Cars, answered Eric.

Oh yeah! Yo Dave, "Pass me da dime bag so I can roll up another fat one," said James in his worse Jamaican accent. What about cars?

You said you need a car to get a girl.

Damn! This weed makes a nigga forget shit sometimes. Anyway, you don't exactly need a whip. It just makes things easier, proclaim James.

I've gotten numbers without a car.

The three of them turn and look at Eric, like he was Bill Clinton saying he didn't have sex with Monica, seeing right through his lie.

Ok then, tell me something? How far do you get wit dem? How much money do you have to spend and how much time do you put in, asked James interrogating him.

Eric sits there in complete silence, assuming they know he's lying.

See, with a whip you don't have to do all that shit.

You get any pussy yet, asked John.

Already feeling embarrass, he still doesn't say a thing.

Don't lie mutherfucker, cause you know I know, said Dave.

So what, I'm eighteen and still a virgin. Is that a crime?

It's fucked up, that's what it is, laughed John. Look at you. You six foot, dark-skinned, skinny, baby fro scared of women muther-fucker.

So what! I admit I'm slow when it comes to women and street life.

If you're a virgin, why the hell are you arguing the knowledge we're droppin' on you?

Your brother, said James, pointing in Dave's direction, has a whip and the phone stays ringin' off the hook.

It's not ringing now, mumbled Eric with his head down.

Shut up, said John, throwing the dice at him that were laying on the table in front of him.

It's not ringing smart ass cause I have the ringer turned off so we won't be interrupted, answered Dave. Check out how many messages are on my answering machine.

Eric looks over, and sees eighteen.

They're probably all from Pam, whispered John.

What faggot? I heard that, turning his head in John's direction.

Don't front nigga, like she ain't always blowin' up ya line.

Fuck you! Don't hate cause I passed where you failed, you jealous pussy.

Failed, he responding harshly. I didn't want that hoe, that's why I passed her on to you.

What? Please all you get is left overs.

Both of y'all need to chill, cause the bitch ain't worth it, said James trying to be the peacemaker again.

They stare at each other for a moment in complete silence and then begin laughing as if they were sharing an inside joke.

E, you know what goes on around here. Don't doubt what I tell you.

Can I finish, said James, before I forget again?

Go ahead, replied Dave. You need to stop smoking that shit so much. Were gonna start calling....Who was that character Chris Tucker played in Friday?

Smokey! Said Eric.

Yeah Smokey! Do you smoke while your working? Driving that delivery truck droppin' off auto parts. They have to smell that shit on you. You probably sweat that shit out your pores.

Anyway, with a car it makes shit ten times easier. Said James, turning his attention to Eric.

You don't have to kick much game. You can take them out whenever you feel like it. You can make up for lost time. And last but not least, you can answer a "Booty call." You don't want to go see a honey late at night on the bus. You might end up missing.

A "booty call" he repeated.

Hell yeah! Ain't nothing like some late-night pussy, joked Dave. But see, if you a true baller like myself, you can get them to come to you, patting his chest in confidence.

So if I hear y'all right, you need money for all these things to happen, so money comes first.

No cause you can also control things with power. Now how many times in school you see a couple of ugly guys who got all the females around them and not have a dime in their pocket?

All the time. I know I got more going on than them.

Don't hate, you know how they do it?

If I did, I wouldn't be here listening to y'all.

Game! To have power, you must know how to kick game.

Well I guess I'll never have power.

Don't give up hope. It takes time to per-fect yo mack. You learn sumthin' new every day.

How do you approach a chick?

I don't, said Eric.

There's your first mistake. You don't have any confidence in yourself. Women can see a mile away that your shy, awkward and weak, which is a turn off. Your not ugly. You just have to learn to stand up straight, keep your chin high and be forceful when you speak.

Look at me! I'm eighteen with pimples all over my face and I don't like rejection.

You have to have a plan. Like a guy is about to shoot you and you have to talk your way out of it.

What do I say?

You have to pay attention to every little detail, from body movement to facial expressions. Tell her what she wants to hear.

Like what?

Good things. Lie, if you have to. Tell her she's pretty even if she isn't or that you like her hairstyle when it looks jacked up.

She might not believe me.

That's when the game starts with her. She's gonna come off like your full of shit, but if she gives you a smile or number, trust me, your ass is in there.

So females have game too?

Oh yeah, much better then ours. So you always have to be on top of yours. Only answer questions asked and don't give up too much info.

So really it's a chess game being played, stated Eric, starting to make sense of some of it.

Yup! And if you're not careful, you'll find yourself ass out.

So what's next?

I'll take it from here, intervened John. You have to watch out for two things. One is the number game.

What's that all about?

It's like this; if the bitch only wants your number, that means she likes to be in fucking control, call you whenever she feels like it. Now, if she gives you her home and cell number, yo ass is in there. As long as you play yo' cards right.

Eric nods his head in agreement.

Now there's the nigga thing. If she says she has a friend who she just talks to or kick it wit, that means she has a standby dick, but the door is open for a new dick.

But if the bitch comes out and says she has a nigga and still gives you the digits, that means she's feelin' you, but she'll only fuck with you whenever her man is not around or is fucking up. So you have to think, is this pussy worth a beat down or getting shot if yo ass get caught?

Got it! What else?

Don't get caught up in the telephone love syndrome, said James.

What's that?

That's when you call a chick everyday.

What's wrong with that? I want her to know that I like her.

True! But you don't want to sweat her. Look, ain't nuthin' worse then getting locked in an routine.

If you call her everyday, she's gonna expect that shit all the time and don't miss a day or your gonna catch hell. Plus! Don't be one of those fools who calls more then once a day.

Before you know it you spent all day on the phone talking to her "bout nothing".

How many times should I call?

Two or three times a week. Keep her missing you and sweating you, not the other way around.

How long should we talk on the phone?

Maybe an half hour. You don't want to be on the phone long. And always end the conversation when it's going good.

Why do I want to do that?

Always leave her wanting more. Don't wait for the conversation to get boring, then y'all might not want to talk to each other again.

Okay!

I guess it's on me again, said Dave. Let's talk about dating. Don't be no fool and spend all yo cash and get no ass.

So what do I do?

You have to see if she's a fake sister.

A "fake sister," said Eric, never hearing that expressions before.

You have to find out if she likes you for you or what you got.

I ain't got nothing.

You will in due time. Sisters know if you're a nut or got potential. So you have to keep things simple: movies, Mickey D's, dinner every now or then, her house or here. Don't go all out until she's willing to spend her last dime on you or giving up tha ass.

How will I know where she's coming from?

Depends on how long it takes for you to tap tha ass. If you're hitting tha ass before she knows your last name, don't waste your time on her. Treat her like the hoe she is, cause all she's gonna do is juice you for what you got until something better comes along.

While we're on the sex subject, how do I handle it?

You go all out, of course, answered James.

Tear tha ass up, responded John, acting like he's smacking a female's butt.

She should hold back thou, implied James. Every female is a freak, but you want to find out slowly or you're gonna question how many dicks she been wit.

Don't I want her to go all out?

Only if it's a one-night-stand. If she's buffing your helmet and throwing you up against the walls the first time y'all slapping skins, you'd better watch yourself. The right chick knows how to spread that shit out, hittin' you wit something new each time.

What about condoms?

Use them mutherfuckers all the time. You don't want to end up dead or a baby daddy.

Yo' fuck that shit, spited John. If she's all that, raw dogged-style nigga. If you want to feel how good it is, acting like he's doing it doggy style.

What you got to say bro?

That's tricky, said Dave rubbing his chin. You should use them all the time in this day and age, with A.I.D.S. spreading at a high rate or you could end up being a baby-daddy. But sometimes you don't want to fuck up the mood. But you better hope she is taking some kind of birth control, because you won't have the power to pull out like I said before, trust me, I know.

"You got a girl pregnant"?

Almost, false alarm. But I was sweating bullets.

Don't believe his ass, said John. I'm sure he has a few little ones running around somewhere. They just haven't found him yet.

My address and number is still the same, stated Dave, responding to his comment. So if I have any babies out there, their moms know where to find me. I don't run from responsibility.

What's that suppose to mean?

Take it anyway you want.

That baby ain't mine; I don't care what anybody says.

Tell the baby that when it grows up.

Another ghetto bastard, said James.

Fuck all y'all, hollered John, raising his middle finger.

Eric attempts to speak, but he is quickly cut off. Don't even go there, mumbled John daring him to ask a question about the situation.

I wasn't going to say anything, retreating his comment.

Everyone gets quiet for a moment, letting things cool down as John starts to think back about Shelia. His so-called baby-momma he met two-years-ago while working for an department store. She was the manger, in her late thirties who hired him. She only hired him because of his looks, which usually suckers the women in, until he opens his foul mouth, then they don't want no part of him. She could tell he was a bad boy which turned her on.

He knew she was feeling him and he use it to his advantage, coming to work late all the time and stealing right in front of other employees. Every time he was summon to her office to answer the allegations, he would knock her off and she would forget about everything. Other workers knew what was going on, because he would bragged about it, but nothing was done. She would buy him clothes, give him money, let him stay over and drive her car. Everything was lovely for him until three months down the line she called him to the office to discuss a certain matter. He was prepared to knock her off again, but she surprise him by saying she was pregnant. Of course he denied it, but he knew it was his. He told her he needed time to think about what they were gonna to do and never came back to work. She knew he wasn't right for her and couldn't provide for them so she just left it at that.

Trying to change the subject, Eric asked his brother another question. Bro, how will I know who is Mrs. Right?

You'll forget about everything we told you, an' you'll be walking around here wit your head on backwards doing every and anything to please her. You'll start thinking twice about everything you do and how she would feel about it. Basically you'll develop a conscience and then we won't see yo ass anymore. In other words, you'll ass be whipped. That's why you practice on the Ms. Wrongs to prepare yourself for Mrs.

Right. I haven't found her yet, so that's why I do the shit I do. Plus you're still young. You don't want to be tied down.

Why not?

Cause there's plenty of shit out there to do, said John jumping in.

Like, responded Eric.

Like traveling, hanging out, sleeping with as many bitches as you can, having two girls at once or a fucking orgy.

Orgy, shouted Eric, like a kid walking in a candy store with his eyes bugging out of his head.

Yo, remember when we did that shit y'all? Matter of fact, it was down here, said Dave.

Here! Where was I?

It was that time when you, Moms, and Dad went down south.

Next time I'm staying home.

It was a freak feast up in here that day. A smile widened across John's face as he leans his head back looking up at the ceiling reminiscing about what took place that night with the strippers they invited over. See, if you're tied down, you can't do that shit. Unless it's on the lo' lo'. And who wants to be sneaking around? You don't want to tell some bitch where you're going and what time you'll be back. She'll be calling you every hour, wondering where you at. That shit ain't no fun. You'll think yo fucking ass is a kid again.

Yeah, I guess so, since you put it like that.

See Mrs. Right will put a stop to all that shit. So I'm glad I haven't found her yet. . . .Then again, I had a lot of Mrs. Rights, you know what I mean, bragged James. But you know how I do. I keep my shit on tha low. You know my motto "Bragging creates haters, who in turn bring drama".

So is that everything?

Hell no, that's just the beginning, but you had enough for now. Just remember the little stuff, like you're gonna sleep with a ugly chick, young girl, and most of all, a fat chick somewhere down the line.

Hell naw, not me, snapped Eric.

Don't sleep on the big girl. They give the best loving. I had a few. Now don't get me wrong, I'm not talking about the sloppy type that don't take care of themselves. Wearing shit they shouldn't be wearing, showing all their rolls. I'm talking about the ones that know how to work it, that care about their appearance and always have their hair did. Plus big girls have the sweetest voice over the phone.

You right about that, said James. That's how they get me. And there's nothing wrong with an ugly chick either. They have the best bodies. Your not trying to make her your woman or be seen in public with her. You just want tha ass. Tell her to bring her ass over after dark, then kick her out before sunrise.

They all start laughing.

Don't take what we're saying as being a dog, spoked Dave, cause there are some females sittin' around having the same conversation about men.

So are y'all ready, asked Eric?

For what?

For me to put what I learned into action.

Not tonight, it's late. Plus the places we go, your too young to get in. We'll do something tomorrow. I'm tired as hell.

You know I'm fuck up said, John, lying across the couch. I might be in this spot all night.

Your not by yourself, said James. I'm gonna be in this recliner until daylight.

Eric looks at all of them shaking his head. "And they call themselves players."

WHY WOMEN AND MEN CAN'T BE FRIENDS

1. When she says, "You're such a good listener," he's thinking, "I really wasn't listening. I was just daydreaming about us between the sheets."

2. When she says, "You're such a good friend," he's thinking, "I'm willing to accept that title if it leads to us having sex in the near future."

3. When she says "I wish my man was like you," he's thinking, "I'm probably like him except he's hitting it."

4. When she touch, kiss, or hugs him, he's thinking, "If this doesn't lead to us slapping skins, don't tease me."

5. When she goes out of her way for him, like sneaking to call him, doing favors, or hanging out, he's thinking, "She must really like me; hopefully it leads to sex."

6. When she buys him a gift, he's hoping it leads to sex.

7. When he pays for her food, he hopes sex is the thank you.

8. When he makes a sexual joke and she plays along, he's not joking.

9. When her man is acting foul and she calls her so call male friend, he's thinking, "This is a window of opportunity."

10. When she says I'm glad it's not about sex with us, he's thinking, "It is, but I'm willing to wait because my girlfriend is fucking me."

CHAPTER 2
Gametime

It's a Saturday afternoon and the fellas decided to go to the mall to see how Eric handles a real situations.

We're here! Now what, asked Eric, looking around the mall surveying the scene.

Be patient E, just let things happen, answered Dave.

Where you wanna go first, asked James.

I need some new music, let's hit Music Sound, replied Dave, beginning to walk toward direction where the store is located.

Hey bro, where's John?

He had to work.

As they walk through the entrance of Music Sound Dave bumps into a young lady who looks the spitting image of Nia Long heading in the opposite direction.

Excuse me, I'm sorry.

Oh, I'm sorry too, she responded.

As their eyes cross paths, both of them hold their glance while walking away.

Damn man, said James, who noticed the incident.

What?

That's the first time I've seen you speechless.

She caught me off guard.

That never stopped you before.

Whatever! I'm going over to check out the new releases. Come on, E.

I'll be over in the Jazz section, said James.

Hey Eric you see anything you want? Said Dave, bumping him with his shoulder.

I don't have any money on me.

I got you.

Let me see if there's anything I like.

While he sorts through the music items, Dave is glancing around the store.

I want you to look up slowly, said Dave whispering in Eric's ear.

Eric slowly looks up out the top of his eyes, with his head down.

What am I looking at?

See those two over there?

He looks around. Where?

Those two over in the hip-hop section.

Those two girls? What about them?

They've been checking us out since we walked in.

How do you know?

Dave gives him a weird look, not believing his brother is doubting his skills on reading women's body language.

Come on man, it's me. Just follow my lead. They walk over to the ladies and ease up behind them.

Can I help you ladies, said Dave in a smooth deep baritone.

They both turn around reluctantly, acting like they didn't notice them walk over.

Do you work here? The short one with long jet-black hair, light brown eyes, full lips, and a nicely shape body asked.

No, but I can still help you.

How you figure?

I know a lot about music. What's hot and what's garbage.

You know music like that?

That and other things, giving her a crooked smile like Snoop. My name is Dave. And yours?

Mamie! This is my girl Dana. Dana stood about five-foot-four, light-skinned, with blond braids hanging down to her ass, long fake nails, fake blue contacts, a belly shirt that barely covers her big breast, and pants so tight it's a wonder she could breath, fitting the stereotypical image of a chicken head.

How you doing Mamie, Dana? This is my brother Eric, he announce while giving him a nudge. Eric quickly raises his hand and says "Hi" in a low tone.

So Mamie, what type of music do you like?

Hip-hop all night long, she responded, doing a little dance.

Let's take a look down this end of the aisle and see what we can find that's hot. Dave puts his hand on her back and leads her away.

Where you going? Said Dana, reaching for Eric's arm stopping him from following.

With them.

I'm not looking for anything. Stay here and keep me company.

Okay!

So where do you live sweetie? Dana inquired.

The Hills, and you?

Oh, y'all high class. We live in the Bottoms.

Awkward silence looms for a moment, because people from the Hills don't usually deal with people from the Bottoms.

I really don't hang out down there.

I'm sure! You're kind of cute. How old are you?

Eighteen! What about you?

A lady never tells her age. You have a girlfriend?

No, I don't.

Good, cause I'm gonna make you mine.

He is taken aback by that statement.

Meanwhile Dave and Mamie are getting acquainted.

You don't really need to buy anything, mentioned Dave. I'm sure whatever you want I got at home. My music collection is ridiculous.

Really? So you're gonna hook me up, she asked.

You can come over and copy whatever you like.

That's cool, when?

You and your girl can come over tonight.

We just met.

Right! And I'm trying to get to know you better.

You gonna keep your hands to yourself?

He looks at her body, "Hell naw", looking her up and down. Which sends her into laughter.

Ten minutes later they walk back over smiling and laughing like two old friends reunited.

Is everything cool over here, asked Dave.

Yeah, your brother was just keeping me company.

Hey E! Mamie and Dana are gonna swing by tonight, if it's cool with Dana.

Only if it's cool with Eric. All heads and eyes turn and focus on him.

I guess it's okay.

All right, it's set. I gave you my number, so we'll see y'all tonight. Any problems, just call.

All right, tonight, smiled Dana.

Bye, Mamie!

Bye, Dave, Eric!

See, now was that hard? Resting his left hand on Eric's shoulder.

What's gonna happen tonight?

Whatever you want, if you do right and don't mess up.

James walks back over.

I saw y'all pimpin', so what's up?

They're coming over tonight, replied Dave.

Y'all got them freaks coming over tonight, he said with excitement, I'm there.

Naw man, this is all Eric. We'll fill you in afterwards.

Com'on, it ain't no fun if your homies can't have none.

I don't think I'm ready, said an unsure Eric.

Dave pulls him in closer, "You're gonna become a man tonight."

What'cha mean?

You know what I mean.

We just met them.

We can get that pussy easy. They from the Bottoms.

How do you know?

Just trust me, all girls down there are freaks. Let's head over to the food court, I'm starving.

Five minutes later they arrive at the food court.

What'cha y'all want to eat, asked Dave?

I see what I want right there, James responded. Looking at light-skinned chick working behind the register at one of the fast-food spots.

20

Yeah, she's pretty, looks kind of young. You sure you want to mess with that?

I can handle her ass.

Will see.

I'm gonna get in her line.

Me too.

I don't think so. Get in the other line or go somewhere else and order. I know your ass.

I'm just messing, I know how you like to do your shit in private, said Dave laughing as he walked away.

Can I take your order sir, she asked James.

Can I get a small order of curly fries and a large coke.

Will that be all?

I would also like to take you out sometime. What's your name?

She blushes and lowers her head in a shy matter and said "Crystal".

Crystal my name is James. I don't want to hold up the line so do you have a number I can call you at so we can talk.

No, but you can give me yours.

Okay, no problem. Give me a pen and paper so I can write it down.

Here you go.

He writes his name and number down, you make sure you call me.

I will.

He starts to walk away.

You forgot your food, she shouted.

Thanks baby, cause I'm definitely hunger.

As their sitting, eating at a table in the food court, John walks up out of the blue and joins them.

I thought I would find y'all niggas over here. Slapping Dave on the back.

You have fun at work, Dave asked.

Man, I left that bitch early, it was boring.

Don't say shit when your ass gets fired from another job.

Fuck that job and fuck you, reaching for some of Dave's fries.

While they're sitting there talking about nothing in particular, a young lady, tall and slim with short hair and a honey-brown complexion looking like she should be modeling clothes, walks up to their table.

Hey Eric, she said, sounding excited.

He turns his head around to see who spoke. Hey, how you doing Jenny?

Just fine and you?

I've been okay.

Feels good to be finally finished with school.

That's the truth.

So what'cha doing up here, she asked?

Just hanging out with my brother and his friends.

She looks around the table, "Hey Dave! How you been?

Hi Jenny!

So what you doing up here, asked Eric.

I just got off work. I told you before, I work up here, over there in that ladies clothing store, pointing to her left. But right now I'm up here with the medical center I volunteer for. Where handing out pamphlets on sexually transmitted diseases.

I forgot you did that.

Have any of you been tested for A.I.D.S.

I ain't no fuckin' fag, said John.

I would kill myself if I ever caught that shit, responded Dave.

You don't have to be that extreme. Your life doesn't end.

Maybe not for you.

You should help out sometime Eric.

Maybe!

I have to get going. You still have my number.

Yeah!

Call me, we haven't talked since graduation.

Okay!

Take care and don't forget to call me. Bye. See ya Dave!

They both wave bye.

Damn, who's that dime-piece, asked James, salivating like a dog in heat.

She graduated with me, answered Eric.

And you didn't tap that ass. She was all on your shit, said John.

It's not like that, we're just friends.

The three of them stare at each other, then at Eric, and laugh at his inexperience in reading women and understanding the laws between sexes.

Friends, Friends, shouted James. It's time to teach you some new shit.

About what?

Bro, listen and listen good, spoke Dave. I told you before men and women can't be friends, that shit don't exist.

Well, there's a lot of evidence around this mall to prove you wrong and you know about Jenny and me.

What you see around here is bullshit. And you and her are bullshittin'.

Niggas and bitches frontin' their ass off, stated John.

"You know what I'm sayin," responded Dave, giving John a hi-five.

No, I don't have a clue, said Eric, looking puzzled.

Pussy and dick, answered John. One always wants to get in the other.

What?

Pussy and dick, that shit always gets in the way of friendship.

What the hell are y'all talking about?

John gets real animated, taking over the conversation. Look nigger, either you want to fuck her or she wants to fuck you; it's simple as that. Didn't you want to fuck that bitch you were just talking to?

Her name is Jenny.

Whateva! It's all the same.

And the answer is no.

Nigga please, you like her ass, If you don't want a piece of that ass you're a fucking faggot.

So what, I like her, he answered, getting frustrated, and I'm not a faggot.

All right then, apparently she likes your ass. Don't ask me why. That bullshit y'all talking is a waste of time. Y'all both need to stop playing games and come out and say that shit so you can get all up in da ass.

I have female friends I don't want to have a sexual relationship with and I know they feel the same.

Do you really know? James interjects, waiting for a chance to say anything. Yo, I need a blunt.

I'll be back.

Let the master speak interrupted Dave. Eric turns to his brother. Women aren't like men; we hint and make jokes about fucking to see how they're gonna react. If you ask a woman if she likes you, she'll probably say no. They don't like giving up the advantage. They know they have to keep you on your toes. They have to be sure about their feelings and yours, plus it has to be the right time and place for you to get the truth out of them.

I still don't believe it.

I bet y'all be fucking in two weeks. Well then again, were talking about your slow young ass, said John, so maybe we give it bout a month or never.

Eric turns and gives him an evil look.

Pay attention, said Dave, slapping Eric upside his head. Have you ever been around a girl you couldn't stand, but in time you ended up liking her?

Yeah, that's happened.

It's just human nature. If you're constantly around somebody and y'all talking and bull shitting almost everyday, naturally your feelings, aka dick, takes over, and when the opportunity presents itself and neither one of y'all are frontin', you'll be . . .

Tappin' that ass, laughed John.

How come you think brothers end up fucking fat girls and ugly girls. They're constantly around you, all on your dick like they're one of your homies, and before you know it, you're playing ping-pong with her big ass titties or riding that fat ass. Think about this, everybody's mission in life is to eventually settle down and have a family, right?

Right!

Once your ass tie that knot, your wife is gonna put an end to all that so-called female friend shit. She's not even gonna want you talking to females. The only women in your life will be moms, grandmoms, sisters, aunts, and cousins, first cousins of course and if you're a real man, you'll make sure she doesn't have any niggas in her life and keep her away from your best friend.

Now why would we end up going through all that?

Cause so-called friends end up fucking. Go ahead and tell your wife you have female friends. Know the first thing she'll say?

What?

That's right, what! What can you do or say to them that you can't do or say with me. Then what the fuck you gonna say?

He's speechless.

Exactly, nothing! You'll just be ass out. When Dad was around did you see him with any female friends?

No!

Know why? He fucked them all before he got married. Trust me, I know. He knew Moms was gonna put an end to all that shit.

So what if you're not married?

Then you just trying to fuck the bitch. If you're spending your time and money on a trick, you'd better get some ass out the deal.

Seated at a table right next to them are a group of females ease-dropping on their conversation.

Y'all hear that bullshit they're filling his head with? One of the ladies said, they're going to get his young ass hurt believing that nonsense.

That's a dog for you, said her friend.

I know, but he could be a good brother and they're fucking his head up.

Girl, don't worry bout them, just mind your business.

......Just make sure your ass gets out before you start catching feelings or you'll be a pussy-whipped mutherfucker. Just hit it a few times, depending on how good it is, and then go y'all separate ways, continued John.

That's it? Just use and abuse her like she's nothing? That's not me.

You'd better make it you. Just kick her ass to the curve or she's going to want a relationship or keep you from having another, just out of spite or jealously, said Dave. She doesn't want you to think you can fuck her without some kind of a commitment or consequence. That's when the game switches on your ass. See, it started out as a fuck thing with them, but when they see that's all you wanted, they wanna catch an attitude cause they thought they could play their little games on you and . . .

I can't believe you're listening to this bullshit, said the same lady, jumping in their conversation.

The Fellas turn their heads to see who's interrupting them.
Who the fuck are you?Snapped John.
Who the fuck are you, talking all that bullshit?
Bullshit! We're trying to keep his young ass from being played by silly bitches like you.
Bitch! Who you calling a bitch.
Your silly ass, for not minding yo business.
When you say stupid shit about women, it is my business.
That's how silly bitches get hurt.
Bring it on!
Yo, chill, said Dave. What's your name, sweetheart?
Tanisha!
Tanisha, you have a problem with what we're saying?
Yes, the hell I do.
My name is Dave. This is my brother Eric and of course you met John. Why don't you and your girlfriends pull up a chair and let us hear what you got to say.
Okay, this is my girl Candy and my girl Butter.
Nice to meet you. Say what'cha you got to say.
First of all, men and women can be friends.
Since when? Countered John..
You just shut the fuck up. I have male friends.
No feelings involved? Responded Dave.
Just that brother-sister love.
How do you know?
Cause I know.
See, that's a bullshit answer, interrupted John.
What I tell you before, getting heated at his vulgar mouth.

See now . . .

Dave cuts him off.

John's right, you seem like a very smart girl. But just by that statement right there, I can tell you get your feelings hurt a lot.

Mmm huh, mumbled her girlfriend Candy, shaking her head.

Tanisha turns and gives her that shut your mouth look.

How you figure?

Know what's one of men's greatest attributes, that we can do with a straight face?

What?

The ability to lie. If I have to be all friendly with you and act like I don't like you like that just to get some pussy, so be it. I'm just trying to get you to let your guard down so I can sneak in. Then afterwards, depending on if it was all that, we can say it just happen and go back to bull-shitting, until it happens again. Guys will wait years for pussy as long as their getting it from someone else. If you think sex ain't on their minds, you're gonna get your feelings hurt when they make their move. Because I'll tell you now, just by looking at you, it's on mine.

Looking at me?

Your fat ass and big titties, blurted John, pointing to her body parts. If a nigga ain't tryin' to ride that, his ass is gay.

I'm really going to hurt your friend.

Look, said John, getting in her face. As far as I'm concerned, there are three types of niggas. You got niggas who are fags, and all they want is dick. You got real men, like me of course, who keep it real and get any bitch I want. Then you got them punk-ass bitches who's scared of the pussy, right Eric?

Eric just gives him the finger.

Don't worry about him, baby, said Tanisha. To me you're the only real man at this table.

What's up with your girlfriends? What they got to say? Asked John.

Go ahead and tell them they're full of shit, said Tanisha looking at them.

Candy and Butter look at her wondering if they should say what's on their mind.

Girls?

Well, to be honest, said Candy, I think all men are dogs. So what they are saying is probably true.

Dave and John laugh, because her girls ain't backing her.

Know what, fuck y'all.

Don't be mad at them, laughed Dave, they're just speaking their mind.

Should have minded your fucking business, mumbled John.

Know what? Let's get out of here, before I'm arrested for assault and battery. They get up and leave.

See Eric, Dave pointed out, you're just like her. Now she's all mad cause she knows that shit is true. Her girlfriends proved that. Yo John, I think she likes you.

Fuck you and her. While they're sitting there chatting Dave noticed the woman he bumped into at the music store walking on the other side of the mall.

Yo fellas, I'll be right back. He quickly gets up to run and catch up with her.

Where she at, yelled John, knowing he seen a woman he likes. But Dave pays him no mind.

Reaching the other side of the mall, he loses sight of where she went.

Searching through the crowd of people, he bumps into her.

We have to stop meeting like this, she said.

I don't mine if it gives me the opportunity to talk to you.

Really!

My name is Dave and yours?

Shereen!

Nice to meet you.

Are you stalking me?

Only if you don't give me your number.

Why should I?

Cause I don't want to miss out on something special.

How do you know?

Just a feeling I got when I looked into your eyes at the record store.

Now is that the line you had planned to use on some helpless victim?

No, and by the way things look, you don't seem helpless.

Good observation, cause I'm not.

So can I get your number and maybe we can continue this conversation over dinner?

I have to think about it. So give me yours and maybe you'll hear from me.

Here you go, handing her a business card he uses for his job.

Car salesman!

I sale cars not to far from here.

Another female walks up to Shereen.

This is my sister Karen. Karen, what you say your name was again?

Dave! How you doing, Karen?

Fine! Nice to meet you.

I won't hold you up any longer. Make sure you call me.

Will see!

So take care of yourself, Shereen, Karen.

Bye!

Just as they walk away the fellas walk up.

Yo nigga, yelled John. Who was that?

Don't worry about it.

You chasing pussy now, asked James, who had came back when Dave left.

I told y'all he's slipping, bragged John.

I ain't chasing pussy.

Whatever nigga; let's get outta here.

YOUR BEST FRIEND

1. Don't let your best friend get to comfortable around your man or woman.

2. Don't tell your best friend how good the sex is.

3. Don't give your best friend a key to your place.

4. Don't let your best friend spend the night at your place when your partner is staying there.

5. Don't listen to anything negative your best friend says about your lover, if their single or in a bad relationship.

6. Don't do any cheating around your best friend, they might use it against you.

7. Don't let your best friend tempt you into doing something you might regret.

8. Don't let them know your lovers work schedule.

9. Don't let them be the third wheel when you go out.

10. No threesome.

CHAPTER 3
Putting It On Em'

Later that night, Dave is getting Eric ready for his big night.

Yo E, you ready for tonight?

I guess so, besides myself what else do I need?

These! He tosses him a pack of condoms.

No doubt, said John, agreeing.

C'mon on, we just met them.

You know how to put one on.

Yeah! I've been practicing in private.

Good! You always have to be prepared, said Dave. Look! Since this will be your first time, let me give you some pointers.

Like what?

Be patience and take your time. If you get to excited it will be over before you start. I'm sure it's not her first time, so let her lead.

What'cha mean?

Let her go first. Let her ride you, until she can't no more. And don't move with her or you gonna bust. Just grip her ass or titties and go with the flow.

Then?

Once she wears herself out, you can do your thing. Since this will be your first shot, do missionary.If you try and hit her phat ass from the back, your gonna cum quick. If you feel yourself getting excited, stop, relax your breathing and do something else.

Like what?

Start kissing her from head to toe, that will waste some time or give her a massage. Just don't eat the pussy. I don't care if she sucks your dick. Save that shit for someone special. And don't forget to put that condom on. Cause bottom chicks always trying to trap a brother with a baby for a free ride. I don't want to see you on some talk show.

Fuck all that interrupted John. When them bitches get here, you tell her to drop to her knees and suck yo dick. While she's doing that you grab a fist full of her hair and make sure she swallows yo shit. After she's done drinking babies, you tear them panties off, bend her ass over the couch and fuck her until she bleeds or can't scream anymore. Once yo ass is done, fuck talking and cuddling, smack her on tha ass real hard, throw her clothes in her face and tell her to get the fuck out. Put yo foot in her ass if she moves to slow.

Yous' a crazy ass nigger, laughed Dave.

I treat'em like they want to be treated. She's a ho giving up the ass and don't know shit 'bout you.

You right about that.

Where y'all moms at?

Atlantic City, she'll be there for the weekend.

What time the ho's coming?

Shit if I know. Hey Eric, where you going?

I have to run to my room to do something.

At the same time Eric runs upstairs, the phone rings.

John, get that for me?

Yo, who this? He barked in the phone receiver.

Yo, what's up, said James on the other end.

Where you at nigga?

I'm going over shorty's house I meet at the mall, so I'll hook up with y'all whenever. Peace!

Peace, clicking the cordless off and tossing it on the couch.

Who was that, asked Dave.

James, he's bout to go fuck some shorty, but fuck him. Where's the pussy?

Why are you worrying about it? Only two girls are coming.

What, responding with a look of dismay on his face. You didn't hook me up?

First, you didn't ask me to. Second, your not suppose to be here.

Damn, that's fucked up. I'll just take Eric's bitch. He won't know what to do with it.

Ain't no shit like that happening. I advise you to think of some ho to call.

While they're arguing over a freak for John there's a knock at the basement door.

They're here!

Dave walks over and opens the door.

Hey what's up?I see you remembered to come the back way.

Yeah, what's up baby, said Mamie walking in.

How you doing, Dave? Where's my cutie at, asked Dana.

Upstairs! This is my buddy John. John, this is Mamie and Dana.

Hey, he said, barely lifting his head to acknowledge them.

Is Eric coming down?

I guess so.

Well, I'm going upstairs to get him.

Be my guest.

You have any problems finding the place, wondered Dave, looking at Mamie?

I'm here.

Yes you are, looking all good, as he spins here around looking her up and down.

Meanwhile Dana found her way upstairs to Eric's room and knocks on his bedroom door,before entering.

You're here, said a stunned Eric.

Yes I am, and why are you up here?She asked curiously.

Oh, I was coming.

You shouldn't keep a lady waiting.

Are you ready to go back down?

Downstairs for what? There's plenty of things for us to do in here.

Like what?

You'll see, as she closes the door.

In the basement Dana and Dave continue their conversation.

I hope Dana doesn't hurt my brother.

I hope so too. He seems kind of slow.

When it comes to women and street life, he is.

How come?

He was sheltered. Our Mom wouldn't let him do shit. Our cousin died hanging around the wrong crowd. He got shot so she doesn't want the same thing to happen to him.

I'm sorry. What about your Dad?

He died a few years back from cancer. You want something to drink, he asked trying to change the subject.

Yeah, what do you have?

I have all the shit.

Good, then mix me up some wild shit. I want to get fucked up.

I don't believe I'm sitting here by myself, mumbled John. Dave, get me something to drink too.

Get the shit yourself.

Fuck you! Hey May...May?

Mamie, she answered, rolling her eyes at him.

Whatever! You have any other girlfriends that might come over?

Nope!

Nobody, I feel awkward.

And you should, said Dave, butting in.

John just stares at him real hard.

Dave walks over and whispers in Mamie's ear while handing her a drink. Hook him up with anybody. It doesn't matter who, tall, short, fat, skinny, missing one leg.

Okay I get it, cutting him off while giggling. I do know one girl, she does my hair.

John jumps up, preparing to leave.

Hold up, we got somebody for you.

Call this girl up. She might be home. She writes down the number on a piece of paper and hands it to him.

Is she all that?

Call her up.

Dave, pass me the phone.

Here, take that shit upstairs. We got things to get into down here.

Back upstairs in Eric's bedroom Dana is preparing to slowly seduce him.

I wanna listen to some music. What do you have we can listen to?

They're over there in that black case, he answered, pointing to the corner.

She walks over and looks in the case. You have all the jams.

Most I stole from my brother.

I'm going put this reggae shit on. She puts it in the stereo and she starts dancing seductively, looking him in his eyes. Am I turning you on?

Staring at her in amazement at how she is moving her body, he can feel himself rise.

Come on, dance with me, pulling him up off the bed.

I don't know how.

Just move your body with mine, putting her ass to his crotch area.

I see someone is ready.

While their upstairs and Dave is handling his business with Mamie, John is trying to set something up for himself.

Can I speak to T? He asked the female caller on the other end of the phone.

This is she. Who this?

Your girl Mamie told me I should give you a call.

Mamie? You must have it going on for her to give you my number. So what's up?

I thought . . . right when he was about to tell her to come over, the other line clicks.

Hold on, said John.

Hello?

Dave is that you?Spoke the female caller.

No, John!

Hey Johnny. It's Pam. Put Dave on.

He's busy.

Doing what?

He doesn't respond.

Just tell him I got off work early and I'll be over.

No, don't, he blurted out. I mean yeah, come on over. He has a surprise for you.

Yeah, I'll be there soon, bye.

After she hung up he starts reminiscing about the times they shared together and how close they were, until she met Dave and things fell apart. Pam is the only person he truly has love for. Ever since she move across the street from him back in his high school days. He spotted her helping her parents carry in their belongings and instantly fell for her. So he took it as a opportunity to introduce himself by going over and helping them. They hit it off and became real close. She would hang out at his house, he would hang out at hers. He showed her around the neighborhood. Then he made the fatal mistake by introducing her to Dave and James. It was love at first sight for her, but for Dave just another notch on his belt. Eventually she stop hanging out with John and started spending more time with Dave, which played a part in John's attitude towards women and added more towards his jealously of Dave. One day at her house when her parents weren't home, he tried to make his move by kissing her. But she quickly turned him down and told him that she has never seen him as more than a friend.

Oh shit! Clicking back over, you there?
I was about to hang up on your ass.
Your voice sounds a little familiar.
Yours does too.
Anyway!I'm over my nigga's house. He's chillin' wit yo girl right now.
What y'all got a little sumthin, sumthin going on?
Something like that.
You want me to swing over there?
Naw, something just came up. I have to step out. But we'll hook up. I'll get back.

Upstairs, Dana starts to make her move.
You like aggressive women, she asked.
Yeah, I guess. It takes a lot of pressure off me, answered Eric.
Good, cause I like being in control.
She pushes him on the bed and starts kissing him on the neck and taking off his clothes in the process.
Are you sure about this? We barely know each other.
What you think I'm trying to do now?
But, I'm saying.
You don't have to say anything, unless you want me to stop.
No! It's just, I'm kind of new at this.

I figured that. Just lay back and let me do my thing, cause you gonna feel something you never felt before.

A half hour later Pam arrives at the house, using the front entrance.

Hearing a knock at the door, John gets up to answer it.

Hey Pam, he said, opening the door. Come on in.

Hey Johnny, giving him a hug.

Why you come through the front?

I don't like walking around back when it's dark. Where's Dave?

Downstairs waiting on you.

She heads downstairs, hearing slow music and smelling incense, a smile stretches across her face. Reaching the bottom of the steps, she sees a naked women's head in between Dave legs. Lowering her head in disappointment, she turns around and heads back upstairs without being noticed.

Why did you do that? She asked with tears streaming down her face.

I wanted you to see for yourself what type of nigga he is.

I thought he was your friend.

He is and so are you, but I can't stand him playing you, especially when I can treat you better.

I can't believe he would do this to me, plopping her butt down on the couch with her face in her hands.

I told you, you should be with me.

Is that all you're thinking about? I just got my heart broken.

And I can fix it, if you give me a chance.

Give me your forty, reaching her hand out.

You don't drink.

Just give it to me. Snatching it out of his hand and swallowing a big gulp before handing it back.

Want me to walk you home?

If you like. I really don't care at this point.

Hold on, just let me get something out of the kitchen.

While in the kitchen he takes a pill out of his pocket and slips it into the forty bottle before walking back into the room.

Here, you can have the rest of this.

Good, cause I need it.

You sure you can handle it.

Give it to me. She takes another sip. Let's go.

Meanwhile down in the basement, Dave and Mamie are finishing up.

Oh my God, that was the bomb. I can't stop my right leg from shaking, said a excited and exhausted Mamie.

That shit was good, bragged Dave, feeling proud of himself. My fridge is empty, I'm gonna check upstairs to see if there's something to eat. You want anything? He asked while throwing his bathrobe on and heading upstairs.

Bring me back whatever you have, she hollered.

In Eric's room they stop to take a little breather.

See, you did okay. Now was that hard, asked Dana.

I think I'm in love, he uttered.

Well, lover man, I'm going to get some ice cause I'm not finished with you yet.

Want me to get it, he suggested eager to please her.

No luv, just be ready for when I come back. She gets up, puts on his t-shirt and heads downstairs.

John must have left, wondered Dave, looking around, as he walks in the kitchen. He then proceeds to grab an empty cup and fill it up with ice.As he sucks on a ice cube, Dana walks in.

Oh, I didn't know anyone was down here.

Looks like everybody got lucky tonight.

Eric was the lucky one.

And so was Mamie. She might need your help walking home.

Your brother might not snap out of his coma.

I hope you didn't put it on him too bad, he laughed.

I tried not to, but lets see can he hold up for another round.

You're not finished yet?

I've just begun.

Damn! I don't think your girl can handle any more.

She might not, but I can, inching closer to his face. And give a lot.

Flustered by her statement, an awkward feeling starts coming over him.

It's getting hot. I need one of these cubes to wipe across my forehead.

Sure! She reaches in his cup for a piece of ice. Oops, dropping it on the floor. I'll get it.

She turns around, bends over to pick it up causing her shirt to rise up showing her ass.

Then she puts it between her lips and slowly sucks on it and puts it back in his cup.

Ain't nothing prettier than that, she said before turning around and walking away.

She ain't no good, he said shaking his head.

Meanwhile outside Pam's apartment she is trying to maintain her balance while searching for her keys in her pocketbook.

You okay, asked John.

I think so. Thanks for walking me home, I can take it from here.

She step up on the first step and loses her balance.

See what happens if you're not a drinker? Let me get you upstairs. Putting her arm around his neck, he takes her up to her apartment.

Thank you. My head is spinning.

He leads her to the door, takes her keys, opens the door, and guides her to the bedroom.

Here, let me lay you down in your bed.

Okay I'm going to sleep n— She drifts off to sleep before completing her sentence.

Yeah, you do that, while I do my thing, he mumbled in a low tone.

After ten minutes pasted with her laying there motionless he begins taking off her clothes and starts having his way sexually with her.

Finally, after satisfying his sexual craving, he puts his clothes back on so he can hurry out of the apartment.

Damn, girl, you should have been awoke for that. It was good. Sleep tight while I step.

As he opens the front door to leave he bumps into her roommate, who was about to enter.

Oh! Hey Kelly, said a startled John.

What are you doing here, she asked.

Pam wasn't feeling well, so I brought her home.

Where's Dave?

He had an emergency, so he couldn't do it.

Right, knowing something strange is up.

Why do you always act like a bitch, he snapped, getting defensive.

Only to you. Do I need to remind you about a certain incident? Recalling the time when he raped her.

Bitch, please, you wanted that shit. Anyway, your girl is asleep so don't wake her. He pushes past her on his way out.

The next day after a pleasurable night Eric is all smiles, entering the kitchen, where Dave is seated at a table eating a bowl of cereal.

Hey bro' thanks!

For what, looking at Eric strange.

Last night was all that.

Wonder why you waited so long?

Never again. She's coming by today.

Today!For what?

For more of this good stuff, reaching down grabbing his crotch.

Oh, you think you're the man now, laughing at him.

That's right!

Just slow down lover boy, you don't want to fall in love with it.

With what?

The pussy.

She's special.

Every person says that there first time, until they experience others.

Right!

Damn, he's caught up already. I don't want to hurt his feelings. E, just don't give her the world just yet.

Your just jealous, because I got the better looking one.

Dave looks at him like he lost his mind, then he looks down at his watch on his wrist.Shit,I'll talk to you later.

That's if I'm not busy, answered Eric.

Later that day, as promised, Dana stops by to see Eric, who is overcome with excitement as he rushes to open the front door to let her in.

I'm here, said Dana with her arms out extended for a hug.

Happy to see her, he lunges at her and kisses her on the lips. I made you a little something to eat.

The only thing I'm hungry for is you. Slowly she easing him back, then pushing him down on the couch and continues kissing him."Come on, let's go upstairs, she whispered in his ear."

After having another love session in Eric's room, she puts her plan in effect.

Dana?

Yes, baby?

I love you.

I love you too.

You do?

Yes baby? Can I ask you something?

Yeah!

Never mind. Acting hesitant as part of her game.

What?

I need a favor.

What? Anything for you.

Could I get fifty dollars?

Fifty, of course, he responded without hesitation. I have money saved up. I'll give it to you before you leave.

I'm about to leave now.

Now, why?

I have to go pay a bill by a certain time.

You just got here.

I know, but after I take care of some business, I'll be back.

You will?

I promise.

All right. I'll get it.

He jumps up and goes into his secret stash located in his closet in a shoe box and gives her what she wants. She snatches it out of his hand, quickly gets dress, kisses him on the cheek, and leaves without looking back.

BATTLE OF THE SEXES

1. When she wants to talk, he wants her to shut up.

2. Wine and dine to her is beer and chips to him.

3. When she wants to make love, he just wants to bust a nut.

4. When she wants quality time, he wants to watch the game.

5. While she is shopping, he would rather sit in the car.

6. When she wants to be told does she look as pretty as Halle Berry, he wants Halle Berry.

7. When she asks, "Do I look fat in this outfit?" he wants to say "Hell yeah".

8. When she wants affection, his version is slapping her on the ass and saying "Make me a sandwich."

9. When she wants something new, he's looking for the cheap version.

10. When she says "I love you," that's when he loses his hearing.

CHAPTER 4
Black Men Black Women

Welcome to Breakfast All Day. Hi, my name is Sharon. I'll be your waitress. Just two? Smoking or nonsmoking?

Non smoking, they both answered.

Follow me, I'll take you to you table. She directs them to a table located in the far corner. You can have a seat here.

Let me get that for you. He pulls out a chair for Shereen to sit down.

Thank you! You're such a gentlemen, flashing him a pretty smile.

Would you like anything to drink? Asked the Waitress.

I'll have a glass of milk, said Dave. What about you looking at Shereen.

A small glass of orange juice will be fine.

Here you go, handing them both a menu.

Take your time to look it over and I'll be back to take your order.

This is a nice place, stated Shereen, looking around in amazement. I've never been here before. How did you find it?

One of my friends told me about it. I'm glad you decided to come with me.

I never turn down a free meal, she said giggling.

The waitress comes back with their drinks.

Here's your glass of milk and here's your orange juice.

Thank you, he said with a smile.

You're welcome, she said with a flirtatious grin.

Shereen also said thank you, but the waitress walked away, ignoring her.

I seen that, she said.

What, he answered with a puzzle look on his face.

She was flirting with you.

What, that? She's just working for her tip.

Sure! I see I have to watch you.

Me, pointing to himself. What I do?

Do you think she's pretty?

47

She's okay! But not as pretty as you.

Good answer! I thought I was gonna have to throw this glass of orange juice in your face.

Why do females always do that?

Do what?

Ask a man if he thinks another woman is pretty. Only a stupid guy would say yeah.

So you do think she's prettier then me.

Knowing whatever answer he gives is the wrong answer, he just keeps his mouth shut.

It's okay to say yes. I won't get mad reaching for her glass of orange juice and taking a sip.

"Sure you won't." he mumbled lower enough that she couldn't hear him. She's okay, like I said, but not as pretty as you, grabbing and caressing her hand.

A smile stretches across her face.

Well, I think she's pretty.

See, females can do that.

Do what?

Judge other women. If a guy thinks another guy looks good then he must be gay.

Why does it have to be like that?

It's the men's "Code Of Honor".

"Code of what?" covering her mouth trying to keep from laughing out loud.

Code of Honor!It's certain rules real men live by.

What rules?

Like you don't judge another man looks. Unless he's as ugly as Flavor Flav.You sit every other seat when you go to the movies with your homies. Knowing how to keep your feelings in check.I can go on and on.

Men are a trip.

I know you don't understand. Women are to emotional.

And guys like to be macho, afraid to act like you care about something, so you won't be considered soft.

You have us all figure out.

When was the last time you cried?

I'm not sure, looking up at the ceiling to avoid answering the question, suddenly the waitress comes back, saving him.

Excuse me!

Are you ready to order?

Go ahead Shereen, you can order first.

I'll have the number one special and a refill on my orange juice.

Number one, that's three hot-cakes, sausages, and how would you like your eggs?

Scrambled.

And you sir, she asked smiling and batting her eyes in a flirtatious way, while waiting for his response.

I'll have the same.

Your eggs?

The same.

Would you like a refill also?

Please, if it's not a problem.

For you, no problem at all, reaching across him grabbing his empty glass so he can smell the scent of her white diamonds perfume on her neck before walking away with a hard switch in her hips.

"Would you like me to leave?" Shereen interrupted, waving her hand in front of his face to get his attention, as his eyes were focus on her ass.

Com'on, I'm just being nice.

Sure you are.

How come when a female is polite to a guy it's okay. But when a man is nice, it's a problem.

Problem? I didn't say there was a problem. You must have a guilty conscience.

A Awkward silence looms, as he wonders if the date is taking a wrong turn.

Hey, you think you're slick, throwing her napkin at him.

Now what did I do?

You never answered my question.

What question?

You know what question. When was the last time you cried?

Oh that question, rolling his eyes.

Yeah, that question.

The last time I cried was when I was eleven.

Over a girl.

Hell naw, cause the Transformers cartoon was cancelled.

You're so stupid, laughing at his answer. I think that's why I like you.

Cause I'm stupid.

No, cause you make me laugh, like now, silly.

How is school coming along?

Good!

What's your major again?

Psychology!I have one more year left.

Why you pick that?

I love helping people, especially children.I feel any problem can be solve if you get to the root.

Yeah, there's usually a reason for everyone's problems.

I just want to stay focus.

I'm just happy I was able to convince you to go out with me.

I can't have you thinking things will come easy with me.

They sit there talking to one another and don't notice a half-hour has passed before the waitress finally comes back over with their order.

Here's your food.

Thank you, said Dave. But Shereen remains quiet.

If there's anything else you need just let me know, touching him gently on the shoulder before she goes the opposite way.

It's cold at this table.

If she wants to be rude, I can too.

He looks at her and shakes his head, laughing at her jealously.

Let's eat, reaching for his fork.

"Stop" she yelled, smacking his hand.

What was that for?

We have to say grace. Bow your head.

He slowly bows his head while she says grace.

Amen, said Shereen.

Amen reluctantly comes out of his mouth. Now, let's eat!

She chuckles, watching him dive into his food.

All of a sudden they turn their heads to the right, over hearing a couple arguing, disturbing everyone.

Why do you always have to get loud? An older African-American gentlemen yelled.

You're the one getting loud, answered the African-American woman sitting across from him.

You always like starting shit in public places.

Fuck you! If your stupid ass didn't say dumb shit, we wouldn't be arguing.

Fuck you bitch, throwing his fork down on the table.

Bitch, bitch, your momma's a bitch.

Why you have to bring my mom into this. I'll slap the shit out of you, raising his hand above his head.

You started it, and if you touch me, I'll get your ass locked up.

Shereen shakes her head in disgust. What's wrong with black men and women these days we can't seem to get along.

We're getting along okay.

It's still early. There's still a lot of things we don't know about each other.

Like what? I told you everything about me.

I hope not. I like a little mystery to a man. If there's nothing else to learn about you, then our relationship is gonna be kind of boring. I know there are still some things. I know you have skeletons in your closet.

More like a graveyard, he whispered. Why do I have to be the one hiding something? What about you?

What about me? I know I haven't told you everything about me. I want to keep you on your toes. Right when you think you have me figured out, I'll hit you with something new.

So you like playing games?

No, I just like keeping things new and exciting.

See there's another difference between men and women.

And that is?

See guys like to get right to the point, put everything out there all at once, whereas women like to drag shit out I mean things. Trying to watch his language, remembering their phone conversation about how she doesn't like cursing. Give a little bit at a time.

It's not dragging sh...biting her tongue.

Caught you, pointing at her.

I mean things out. It's about romance and building suspense. That's a way to a woman's heart.

That's fine with me. But y'all want that shit all the time. Like today for instance, I brought you flowers.

Yes you did, and I love them.

That's good. I'm glad you appreciate them. But now every time we go out you're gonna expect that shit all the time.

Can you please stop cursing? I don't like that. You can get your point across without all the profanity.

I'm sorry, force of habit.

I'm not the type of woman who expects something from a man every time I see him. I might surprise you and bring you some roses; everybody is not the same. You have some good and bad women and some good and bad men.

Which one am I?

It's like this, If you're one of the bad ones, you won't be with me for long.

See, that's what I like about you. You know what you want out of life and your man.

Well, I owe that to my parents. They raised me to speak my mind, not settle for less and to make something out of my life.

That's good, because all the girls I seem to run into are chicken heads, who just want to be with me for what I got instead of who I am.

Who are you?

A strong black man, raising his right arm to he side and flexing his bicep muscle.

Put your skinny arm down. Men always want to show how strong they are.

Cause y'all like a strong man who can protect you.

A strong man to me is a man who's not afraid to show his emotions and who is willing to walk away from a fight.

Damn, you're different.

Really, you think so.

Really! Don't take what I'm about to say the wrong way. But all of my relationships have just been about sex. And the heart that was getting broken was theirs. I never open myself up to anyone.

You're doing it now.

I know, and it's weird. I told you there's something about you I like.

Why should I believe you? How do I know that I'm not just another trophy or challenge?

You know you're not or you wouldn't be here with me.

So true.

But don't front and act like females don't like challenges just like men.

Yeah, but they're different. Guys just like to see how many panties they can get in or poppin' a virgin's cherry.

Some guys.

Don't act like you're innocent.

Well y'all like to try and change a brother to what you want, especially if he's a rough neck. You don't like messing with pushovers. They're too easy; they do whatever you want. No, you want the drug dealer, the brother who's always yellin' at you, the one who calls only once a week and only comes to see you when he wants sex. The one who is in and out of jail or has at least six different baby mammas. The bro—

I get the point, she interrupted. I never had or will I ever disrespect myself by going out with lowlifes like that.

You got plenty of friends that probably will.

I know, like my roommate Lisa. She's seeing this guy who is ten years older than her and still lives with his wife, but told her they're not together and they don't sleep together.

You know that's bullshit.

Oh, I know, plus he hits her.

Now see, that's out, I would never hit a woman.

I hope not. If you ever raise your hand to my face, I'll kick your ass.

Watch the language.

Shut up Mr. Funny Man. But anyway, that's only one of my girlfriends. I'm not even gonna talk about the rest. They're either dealing with a drug dealer, a blunt head, or a low-life bum, and I'm quite sure some are on the down low. That's why I barely hang around them. I mostly hang out with my little sister trying to keep her on track.

The girl I saw you with at the mall, right?

Yeah!

She's pretty. Is she just like you?

Yes she is.

How old is she?

Eighteen, why?

Maybe we can hook her up with my brother. He's none of those nuts you mentioned.

Maybe! Is he gonna respect her?

Of course. He's my brother.

I know. That's why I asked.

Miss Comedian, smiling back at her.

All a sister wants is a little r-e-s-p-e-c-t.

Hey, I give respect to those who deserve it. Like your roommate, she doesn't deserve it. She doesn't even respect herself.

That still doesn't give you the right to take advantage of her, getting a little upset.

I haven't done anything to her. You need to tell her so-called man that.

He doesn't care, she's just a little sumthin'-sumthin' on the side to him. I tried talking to her, but she doesn't listen. I don't know what to do, lowering her head.

Well if she's really your friend, you just have to keep trying until she listens.

She's been my best friend since the first grade. I really do care about her.

Don't eat yourself up over it.

I'm afraid something bad is gonna happen to her.

No what I think part of the problem is?

What?

No father figure. A lot of these young girls are growing up without a male influence.So when the first knuckle head comes along and shows them a little attention, their all in love, when really she's just a booty-call for him. Then she comes so dependent on him after he destroys her self-esteem, she'll stay with him threw all the bullshit having baby after baby.If they had a daddy around who is treating there mother like a queen, they would know how a woman is suppose to be treated.And that goes the same for the fellas.

I can agree with that, she did grow up without a father. But the mother is at fault to.They're so young nowadays that they don't spend enough time with their child, too busy trying to get their party on.A lot of kids are rasing themselves these days.

Look over there.

She turns her head and sees the couple that was arguing before, now kissing.

Oh that's great they made up.

See, everybody has their problems. It's just how you work them out.

Communication is one way. Without that no relationship will last.

That's the truth.

The waitress returns with the check.

Here's your bill,laying it on the table and walking away, still swaying her hips.

I'm stuffed, said Dave.

So am I.

You barely ate anything.

Don't talk. Look at your plate. That's why you're so skinny.

You still love me though.

I know . . . Sike. Here's my half of the bill.

What are you doing?I got this!Pushing her hand back.

No, you don't have to.

What I say?

Well I got the tip and next time.

Already setting up the next date, can't get enough of me.

Shut up!

You're going to tip her, said a shock Dave.

I guess I'm too nice. Go pay the bill. I have to go to the bathroom and I'll meet you at the front door.

While Shereen goes to the bathroom the waitress approaches Dave.

Hi sexy, she said in a seductive tone.

Hi, he answered. Looking surprised.

What's your name?

Dave!

Well Dave, my name is Sharon, in case you forgot.

I didn't forget.

But my friends call me Puddin'. I don't have long before Ms. Thang comes back.Here's my number. Give me a call and maybe you'll find out why they call me Puddin'.

But I'm with somebody.

Look here, stuffing the piece of paper with her number on it in his shirt pocket and putting her chest in his face.

Once you taste this, pointing to her special area, you'll forget all about Ms. Thang.

Then she turned and leaves. He quickly gets up and heads over to pay the bill just as Shereen walks out of the bathroom.

Are you ready Dave?

Sure, let's go!

As they walk out, he gives the waitress one last look and she blows him a kiss without Shereen noticing.

After spending time with Dave, Shereen finally gets home to her apartment. Lisa, are you here? She called out walking in seeing nothing but darkness.

Mum huh sounds echo in the blackness.

Girl, why are you sitting in the dark? She questioned, gliding her hand across the wall searching for the light switch.

No, don't cut the light on, shouted Lisa.

Oh my God, girl! What happened to your face, looking at the dark bruise mark on her cheek.

I know it's bad, said Lisa, feeling her swallowing cheek with her right hand.

Shereen palms her face in her hands and looks her in the eyes and asked, "Did Wayne do this to you?"

She lowered her head in shame to avoid answering.

I don't understand you. Shaking her head in disgust. Come on, let's go.

Where?

To the hospital, grabbing Lisa's arm.

No, I'm not going anywhere, pulling back emphatically.

Girl, come on, pulling her arm.

No, yanking her arm back again.

Shereen stands there staring at her, debating what she should do.

All right, hold on, said Shereen.

She goes into the kitchen and brings back a bag of ice.

Move over, she sits down next to her. Lay your head down on my lap.

She lays her head down and Shereen puts the ice on her swollen face.

You can't keep going through this, it's getting worse each time.

I know. I'm gonna leave him.

I heard that before.

I will this time, closing her eyes to rest.

When Dave enters the back of his parents house, he is greeted by unexpected guess.

Yo what's up, said James lounging in his bed, drinking a Heineken and flipping channels with the television remote.

Damn man. You scared the shit out of me. What the fuck you doing in here?

You forgot I know where you hide your spare key.

You put it back?

Yeah!

Good, cause I'm hiding it somewhere else.

James just laughs.

I see you made yourself at home. You could at least get your dirty ass sneaks out my bed.

My bad! Where you been?

Out, mom! The question that needs to be asked is "Why are you here?"

Damn, it's like that.

Naw! I'm just tired but I know something up, so spill it.

Alright get yourself settled first and I'll chill over on the couch.
Oh thank you, since this is my spot.

He gets himself settle so James can tell him what's going on.
So what's up, is everything cool, asked Dave.
Remember shorty I meet at the mall.
Yeah, the cashier.
Remember I went to see her that night y'all were with them bottom hoes.
I remember John saying you called.
Listen to this shit I have to tell you.
I'm there.I waste no time getting in the pussy. I'm tearing her ass up on the couch.
Next thing you know, bright headlights are shining threw the windows and she started trippin' screamin'. As he begins recalling the incidents that took place.
Oh my god, said Crystal.
What, responded James.
My parents are home.
So chill, just get dress and will sit here like nothing happen.
There not gonna believe that, plus it smells like sex in here.
What are they gonna do, you're a grown ass women?
You don't understand.
If my dad finds you in here, he's gonna kill you.
Come on, for what?
She gets quiet, debating if she should tell him the truth.
I'm only fifthteen.
Fifhteen, he shouted.
You told me you were twenty over the phone.
I like older guys.
Shit! Quickly putting the rest of his clothes. "Where's the back door?"
In the basement.
The basement, great. Where's that?
Right there, pointing to the door on her left.
I'm out! He rushes over and opens the door and quickly runs down the steps.

But wait, she called, but he doesn't hear her.

That crazy, said Dave.

It gets better, answered James.

I reach the bottom of the stairs and I hear voices around the side of the wall. So I creep slowly to check it out. To my surprise I see some dude banging some chick doggy style. He got her head hittin' the head board. I accidently shouted "Damn she has a phat azz."

Then...

What the fuck, shouted the man turning around to see who is watching.

My bad, responded James.

Who the fuck are you?

Mmm, I'm a friend of Crystal.

The female covers herself.

A friend of Crystal. I'm her uncle, who just got home from the joint this morning and doesn't mind going back. How old are you nigga?

He starts looking for the back door, knowing something bad is about to happen.

I said how old are you, cause if your over eighteen, your dead.

Suddenly James noticed the back door to the far right on the other side of the bed.

Why you moving towards the door? It's not time for you to leave, he starts easing his hand under the bed for his gun.

James noticed him reaching and quickly runs toward the door turns the knob, luckily it wasn't lock, pulls the door open and quickly exiting, never looking back.

I told you she was young, said Dave laughing uncontrollably.

Fuck you!

She's been blowin' up my answering machine since. I ain't calling her back. Let me see if I can pull up my messages from your phone. I'm gonna put it on speaker.

You have ten unheard messages. First message, spoke the answer machine.

James baby, it's Crystal, call me.

What's wrong with that, asked Dave.

Listen, its more.

Second message.....

James, I'm still waiting on your call. Don't worry about my parents, they didn't suspect anything and my uncle kept his mouth shut.

Third message.......

I call you twice yesterday and your rude ass didn't call me back, you better call me or else.

Fourth message.......

You think this is a game, you think you can just fuck me and bounce. I'm gonna have the last laugh. I love you.

You can stop, I heard enough.

You sure, cause there's plenty more.

You got a psycho bitch.

I know! Luckily, all she knows is my first name. I didn't tell her nothing else, not even where I live.

You better stay away from the mall for awhile. Better you then me. This is some funny shit.

Right, for who?

As they sit their laughing a commercial comes on that catches their attention.

My name is Michael and I have A.I.D.S.

My name is Alice and I have A.I.D.S.

A.I.D.S is growing rapidly in the African Amercian community, we account for 38% of most aid cases,57% between ages 25-44, 59% among children. Stop walking in darkness, become aware, turn on the light. Educate yourself and others.

I ain't never catching that shit, said Dave.

Never say never, replied James.

Please, condom stays on my dick twenty-four seven.

Don't act like you never slipped up before.

I gamble sometimes. I look at life like this. When it's my time to go it's my time to go. But it won't be that shit.

Fuck that! I'm trying to live as long as possible.

Anyway, if I did catch that shit, it's a rap.

You would kill yourself.

Hell yeah!

HOW DO YOU KNOW A MAN IS PUSSY WHIPPED?

1. He doesn't hang out with his buddies anymore.

2. He checks in every hour.

3. He can't think for himself.

4. He answers with, "Yes, Dear".

5. He tells the truth.

6. He's depressed until his woman calls him.

7. He goes shopping with his lady and holds her pocketbook.

8. He spends his paycheck on his woman.

9. He can't dress himself.

10. He's always wondering where she at.

CHAPTER 5
Getting Played

The following day John stops by to visited Dave.

Yo, what's up nigga? Said John, coming down the steps.

How you get in here, asked Dave.

Yo' Moms let me in.

You go to work?

Yeah man! Why you always sweating that?

That's the only way your ass stays out of trouble.

Where were you last night? I called you.

I went to bed early.

Yeah, right nigga! Hey, when was the last time you talked to Pam?

Shit, I don't know. She usually calls me every day.

Yo, you treat her like shit.

I know you ain't talkin'.

You know she loves the shit out of you.

Yeah, I know! I never really wanted to cross that friendship line but she kept pushing it. Plus I knew how you felt about her. I'm glad you didn't let it fuck us up.

Yeah, whatever nigga, why don't you call her up?

Why you worrying about her?

That's my girl, pointing to himself.

All right let me see what's up, grabbing the phone and dialing her number.

After two rings a female voice answers.

Hey Kelly, it's Dave. Put Pam on.

There's a brief moment of silence before she responds.

She's not here.

Dave hesitated responding, not believing her answer.

All right, tell her I called, he said before hanging up the phone.

So what's up, said John curiously.

I wish I knew.

Eric walks down the steps.

Hey E, said Dave.

Hey, answered Eric, sounding a little depressed.

You still waiting on that girl to call you? Stop sweating her.

She should have called me by now.

Who? Asked John, butting in.

Dana, the freak from the other night, answered Dave.

You's a pussy whipped mutherfucker.

And a hello to you John, replied Eric, with sarcasm.

That's why I told you to stop calling her. Mamie been blowing up my line but I haven't talk to her since I waxed it.

Yeah man, if she's knows she got you, she'll play your ass and have you doing shit you wouldn't believe, said John.

Like what? He asked.

Giving up your paycheck.

He tries to avoid eye contact to hide his reaction to that statement.

Naw bro', say it isn't so. Don't tell me you're giving that bitch money.

Lowering his head in embarrassment and speaking real low, he answered, "Not much."

How much is not much?

Fifty!

Fifty! They shouted, shaking their heads.

She's playing your silly ass, said John.

Whatever!

Look, interrupted Dave, that's the little money you make sweeping and stocking the shelves for Mr. Johnson's at his store. I know you like her. I'd just want you to watch yourself.

Look, I have a date, so I'm outta here, said John, getting up to leave.

A date with who? Asked a surprise Dave.

That freak I called from here the other night. I'm out.

Don't hurt her.

You know I will, he said before exiting out the back door.

Eric! Shouted their mother from upstairs.

Yes?

There's a young lady up here who would like to see you.

He jets upstairs like a cheetah.

Hi Eric, said Dana with a smile.

Hi Dana, fumbled out of his mouth while trying to catch his breath.

Miss me?

Why haven't I heard from you? He asked showing his temper.

I'm sorry. My mother hasn't been feeling well so I had to take care of her and run things around the house.

Is she feeling better?

I'm here.

Yeah you are.

Let's go upstairs.

Can't, mom's home.

So what are we gonna do?

He tells her to hold on while he quickly runs back downstairs.

Hey Dave?

What?

Can Dana and me chill down here?

With me? Sure, he joked.

Come on man, stop playing.

Just make sure you change my sheets.

Thanks.

He quickly runs back upstairs to get Dana.

Come on downstairs. He grabs her hand and leads the way.

Hi Dave, she said, while walking down the steps.

Hey! He answered, not really paying her atttention.

I'll be right back. I have to run back upstairs, said Eric.

While he runs upstairs, she slowly walks over and stands in front of Dave.

So why are you playing my girl Mamie?

I've been meaning to call her, but you know how that goes, he said with a devilish smile.

Maybe.

So what's up with you and my brother?

You know how that goes, giving him the same smile back.

No I don't. Tell me?

I want to know what's up with you and me, reaching down rubbing her hand across his crotch.

Damn that feels good, he whispered.

I'm back, hollered Eric, running down the steps, skipping every second one.

Dana jumped back quickly, giving some distance between her and Dave.

I gotta make a run. I'll be back later. Said Dave quickly exiting out the back door.

Meanwhile John arrives cross town at the door of the mystery woman he talk to on the phone and rings the bell.

Thirty seconds later a young lady opens the door.

You, said John, with a look on his face like he just drunk sour milk.

What are you doing ringing my bell? Said Tanisha, the female from the mall.

Girl please! I'm not here to see you. I'm here for Tee.

Tee, huh!

Yeah, Tee!

I'm Tee, stupid.

I thought your name was Tanisha.

Tee, Tanisha!

All damn. I was talking to your ass I knew your voice sounded familiar.

There's no way in hell I'm going out with your ass, pointing her finger in his face.

Whatever, bitch, flagging her.

There you go again, just like at the mall. You're in my neighborhood now and your ass better get out of here before you won't make it home.

Fuck you and the bitch-ass niggas around here.

Mike, she yelled upstairs. I got trouble down here.

Who's Mike?

My older brother, so your ass better leave.

I ain't scared.. . . . He looks up and sees about five guys coming down the steps and he quickly wastes no time running the other way.

Thought your ass would leave, she shouted from her doorstep. You'd better not come around here again.

Not happy with the way the phone call to Pam went, Dave decided to make a surprise visit to her apartment.

I'm glad the door wasn't lock, I'm not sure if it she would buzz me in. He said to himself standing outside her apartment door.

Knock, knock.

Coming, a female voice hollered.

She cracks the door.

How you get in the building? Asked Kelly.

Don't worry about it. Where's Pam?

She pauses, and looks over her shoulder.

She's not here!

Why you playing?

I said she's not here. Why don't you go see that other bitch, slamming the door in his face.

Other bitch, what is she talking about?

Trying to figure out what's going on, he starts banging on the door.

I know you're in there.What the fuck are you talking about.

Don't act stupid!

Stupid! Girl, why am I talking to you? Where's Pam?

I said she's not here.

Right!

All that noise you're making I'm sure someone is gonna call the cops. And if they don't, I will.

Fuck you then. What the hell is she talking about? I know she doesn't know about Mamie. Did she see me with Shereen, thinking to himself. Fuck it! I'll go do something else. He heads back downstairs, reaches in his pocket, pulls out some change to use for the pay phone located at the front door.

Hello, Shereen?

Hey David, how you doing?

I'm good. I was hoping to see you.

Aww, I can't!

Why not?

I have to study for a test. Maybe tomorrow.

Tomorrow, sounding disappointed. Okay. I'll give you a call tomorrow.

Bye!

Bye! Fuck it! I'll call Mamie.

Hello, she answered.

Hey Mamie, it's Dave.

What you want?

Damn baby! It's like that?

I been calling you and you never called me back.

I know, and I'm sorry. I've been busy working.

You still could have thought of me.

You right, let me make it up to you?

How you gonna do that?

I'll be by in a minute to get you, so be ready.

Back at the house in the basement Dana is planning to run another scam on Eric.

That was good. You're getting better, trying to hype his ego.

Yeah?

Yes.

I missed you, said Eric.

I missed you too, baby. I was wondering if I could get a few dollars.

Again? I already gave you fifty.

I know, but I had to spend what little money I had on my mother's medicine.

How much responding reluctantly.

Hundred!

What, are you crazy?

I'm sorry, I understand if you don't have it.

I have it, but I can't give it to you.

Come on, please! Don't you love me?

Yes, but a hundred? For what?

There's an outfit I put on lay-away that I need to pay on or the store is gonna to sell it. I don't get paid until next week.

I don't know.

I know how I can change your mind.

She reaches down and grips his penis, puts it to her lips, and starts slowly sucking on it.

His eyes roll in the back of his head from the sensation of never having his dick sucked before which overwhelms him.

Oh, that feels good.

You like?

Oh yeah.

You want me to keep going?

Yes.

Are you gonna give me the money?

Uh huh, whatever you want.

If you get it for me now, I'm going show you a trick I learned with my tongue.

All right, I'll go get it, he jumps up quickly and makes his way to the stairs.

Don't you need some clothes she mention.

For what?

Isn't your mom upstairs?

Oh yeah!

He puts his clothes on and runs upstairs. At the same time, Dave walks in the back door.

Whoa, reacting to seeing Dana lying naked on his bed.

You like, giving him a devious smile.

It ain't nothing I never seen before, he counter.

Trying to ignore how good she looks.

Noticing his hard on, she gets up and walks over to him, grabs his hands and put them on her breast.

Big enough for you?

They're nice. Your girl is outside he mentions trying to keep from giving into temptation.

Mamie's here? I have to see her.

She starts gathering her clothes and getting dressed.

Eric comes running down the steps.

Here's the money you needed.

Money, Dave shouted.

Hey Dave, I didn't know you were back, trying to hide the money behind his back.

I see!

Thank you. She snatches the money out his hand and runs outside.

Hey wait!

She got you again.

She said she really needed it.

We all really need it. You'll learn. Did mom cook?

Yeah.

Go outside and keep them busy while I set something up in here.

You have to change the sheets.

All right, let me see what I can set up on short notice. Trying to set up a romantic atmosphere, he lights some scented candles and place them all around the room, then he runs upstairs and grabs a couple of plates and heats up some fried chicken, mashed potatoes, and some left-over early peas. He then proceeds to head back downstairs to set everything up. This looks good. Looking at the rose in the vase placed in the middle of the table. Now some mood music.

Eric walks back in, hey Dave.

What?

Could I use your car to take Dana home?

Is your stupid ass gonna give it to her?

Come on man.

He throws him the keys, put gas in it.

Tell Mamie to come in.

Thanks man!

Make sure you come straight back. I don't want this girl thinking she's spending the night.

Meanwhile outside, Dana and Mamie are having a conversation.

I'm just playing this fool, bragged Dana, talking to Mamie.

Why are you doing that to him? He seems like a nice guy.

I'm tired of niggas trying to play me. It's my turn.

You ain't right.

Shit, we'll see which one of us ends up with a broken heart.

Right!

Eric walks over and interrupts them.

Hey Mamie, my brother said come on in.

I'll talk to you later, said Mamie, looking at Dana with disappointment.

You ready Dana? He asked.

Let's go, grabbing his arm.

Dave, Dave, Maymie calls in the darkness, where are you?

He sneaks up behind her and covers her eyes with both hands.

Just walk this way guiding her to a table.

What's going on?

Surprise, he shouted, removing his hands.

Wow, is this for me, looking around the room at everything he has set up.

You like?

Yes, giving him a long passionate kiss.

Here, have a seat.

All my favorite foods.

I had this planned. I was just hoping you were free tonight.

You sure this wasn't for somebody else?

Come on girl, I told you I was gonna make it up to you.

Do you really care about me?

I don't do this for anyone.

Dana said you were playing me. She's usually right about things like that.

She just mad because I told her she better not hurt my brother's feelings.

Oh, wondering if she should believe him.

Look, if you want to leave, then go ahead. I would be lying if I said I wouldn't be hurt. If not let's just concentrate on tonight and making it special.

That's fine with me.

How You Know Your In The Friend Zone

1. When she says your such a good friend over and over again.

2. She has no problem changing in front of you.

3. She calls you about her man problems.

4. You're her handyman with no pussy reward.

5. She tells her girlfriends what a nice guy you are.

6. When you talk about taking the relationship to the next level, she thinks your joking.

7. When she's bored, she calls you to keep her company.

8. She calls you her brother.

9. She has no problem talking to another guy in front of you.

10. She ask you if a certain guy is cute.

CHAPTER 6
Stood Up

A few days go by. Shereen is at home studying when out of the blue the phone rings.

Hello, answered Shereen.

How your test go?

I passed.

Congratulation! Why don't I come over so we can celebrate.

I don't know, I have to get up early.

Come on! It's been awhile, I want to see you. You should always make time for self, especially if I'm involve.

Okay, okay! Hurry and get your silly butt over here before I change my mind.

I'm out the door.

Right when she hangs up the phone, it rings again.

Now what you want silly?

There's no response on the other end.

Hello...Hello! I'm hanging up.

Shereen . . . Shereen, a voice finally said in a low tone.

Yes, who's this?

Shereen?

Lisa, is that you?

Help me, please!

What's wrong? She asked because her voice is so weak and she's barely responding. Where are you, she asked beginning to panic, but she gets no response. Lisa, Lisa, hold on, looking at the caller ID. Get Lucky Hotel, where the hell is that? She grabs the yellow book to check. Shit, it's on the other side of town. Hold on girl. I'm on my way.

Fourty-five minutes later Dave arrives at Shereen's apartment. I can't believe she's not answering, he said, standing outside.

He rings the buzzer again.

Where the hell is she? She knew I was coming.

Getting frustrated, he rings it again.

I don't believe this. I told her I was on my way. I know she ain't playing me. Maybe she ran to the store. I'll wait a few minutes.

Hello, can I speak to Dana? Eric asked, the person on the other end of the phone line. Wondering why he hasn't heard from her since he gave her money.

Who the fuck is this? An angry male voice shouted threw the reciever.

Err . . . boyfriend.

Her what? He yelled.

Dana snatched the phone from the man.

Hello?

Dana?

Eric, is that you?

Yeah, who was that?

Don't worry about him. I'm busy right now, I call you later, hanging up before he can respond.

Hello, Hello?

After getting directions, Shereen finally arrives at the Get Lucky Motel.

This place looks creepy, it kind of remind me of one of those cheesy run down one story motels located in the desert all by itself.

She parked and makes her way to the attendants office.

Excuse me, can you tell me what room Lisa Fuller is in? She asked the white man behind the counter watching television.

He checks his sheet.

No Lisa Fuller here.

No Lisa Fuller. She thinks for a moment, how about a Wayne Brooks.

You are? He asked.

His sister, she answered neverously.

You're the second person to ask for him this evening.

Who else?

Some big lady claiming to be his wife and four other huge women with her. I thought they were a gospel group, laughing at his own joke.

Did you tell them?

Hell yeah, they look like they were gonna kick my ass if I didn't.

What room?

107!

I think you'd better call the police, there might be trouble.

Ah shit?

Do you have a spare key?

Yeah!

Grab it.

They rush over to the room.

Knock knock . . . Knock, knock! Lisa are you in there, open up. Lisa! Lisa!

Tired of waiting, she tells him to open the door. He unlocks the door and they proceed to walk in. The TV is blasting, and the room completely destroyed. And they see Lisa bloody and half naked lying on the floor unconscious.

Oh my God!

Quick, call for help, she screamed. Damn girl, I told you to leave his ass alone, getting down on her kness and holding her head in her arms, trying to wake her up. Lisa, wake up, Lisa?

After a long wait help finally arrives.

They're here, he shouted.

Don't worry girl, I'm here with you.

Still standing outside Shereen's apartment, not knowing where she's at or what she's going through Dave finally gives up.

She sold me out again. I need some candy for this sour taste in my mouth.

He opens the glove compartment and a piece of paper falls out.

What's this? Sharon, who's Sharon? Oh, that's the chick from the restaurant. I forgot all about her.

Meanwhile James leaves a wine store located in a plaza a few blocks from the mall carrying a couple of bottles, when he doesn't hear the sound of footsteps approaching behind him as he searches his pocket for his car keys.

Hey sexy, said a soft lovely voice.

He turns around to see who is the familiar voice.

Crystal, he yelled, catching him totally by surprise! Where you come from.

Surprise!

Yes this is a surprise as little beads of sweat start appear on the top of his forehead.

My girlfriends and me, pointing to her left, were just walking back from the mall. I see you have a bottle, planning something special.

Naw! Isn't it past your bedtime, getting sarcastic.

Funny! Well, since you have nothing planned, let's hang out.

After what happen at your house, "Are you crazy".

I willing to let that slide, plus the fact you haven't return any of my calls.

Your to young.

You wasn't worrying about that when you were all up in this young pussy.

I didn't know!

Sure you didn't. She turns around to face her girlfriends. Y'all go ahead, I got other plans.

What you tell'em that for.

Because we got unfinished business.

We do! I don't think so.

I see you want to do this the hard way. You know who my uncle is.

No! And I don't care.

Killer Dre!

Killer Dre the hustler, he responded in shock.

Yes! And now that he's out, he's plans on reclaiming the street. He's hooking back up with his connections and plans on taking out bitch ass niggas to regain control of his territory. And I'm his pride and joy. Anybody fuck with me, get dealt wit. Need I say more.

Whatcha' you want to do, he asked relunctly realizing if he says no, he's dead.

I thought so. Let's go to the back of the art museum and pick up where we left off on the couch.

Get in!

Thought you'd never ask!

THE MYTH ABOUT THE BLACK MAN AND THE WHITE WOMAN

1. She'll put up with your shit.

2. She'll give you head.

3. She's down for whatever.

4. She'll treat you like a king.

5. She'll have your back during the rough times.

6. She'll encourage you when you need it.

7. She'll cook and clean.

8. She'll give you money with no questions asked.

9. She'll buy you gifts for the hell of it.

10. She's family oriented.

11. She'll appreciate the little things you do for her.

CHAPTER 7
The Lighter Side Of Things

The next day . . .

Hey, you heard from that cashier? Asked Dave.

Yeah, I ran into her last night.

You hit it again, didn't you.

James doesn't respond.

Your asking for trouble.

I already got it. Her uncle is Killer Dre.

You want to die.

I'm trapped! If I don't play her game, well you know the rest.

Don't worry, will think of something.

Forget that. Let's talk about this white girl I met at work. I was planning on hittin' it last night until I ran into Crystal.

I don't believe a white girl fell for your bullshit.

Whatever, nigga! Yo, she has an ass like a sister. I mean she's tight from head to toe.

She must eat a lot of Mickey D's. They slap hands laughing at his statement.

Why don't you bring her through, so I can meet her.

Around your ass, I think not!

That's alright. I've fucked a white chick before.

How was it?

I put it like this, I was ready to wife her.

Damn! It was like that. So what happened?

She wanted to be around me twenty-four/seven. She was fucking up the game. Don't let any sisters see you with her ass.

Fuck them! I'm tired of their fucking games.

I feel you on that one.

I'm getting mine from whoever wants to give it to me.

You setting yourself up for some serious drama from the sistas. You know that girl Renee?

The one who talks too much.

Yeah! Well she saw me with a white chick and word got around. I was feeling the heat. I couldn't get pussy from any sister. I had females coming up to me with mad attitude, calling me a sellout.

Come on man! It couldn't have been that bad.

It was, but it was worth it. Believe it or not, she treated me as good as Moms.

Yeah?

It was totally a different vibe. Whatever I needed she was there for me. She even did shit for me without me even asking. She cooked for me and brought me clothes, and she had style. She was breaking me off money. She did all that from the start. She wasn't trying to front like she was down. She was straight white, hockey, rock 'n' roll, the whole nine. You know a sister ain't gonna show her hand until you do it first.

That's true!

She never complained about anything or questioned things I did.

Right!

I'm serious. She treated me good. Whenever we went out she offered to pay.

Fuck all that! How was the pussy?

We did anything and everything you can imagine. She even offer to do a ménage a trios.

Get the fuck out of here.

Trust!

So you saying you would take a white chick over a sister?

To be honest, I don't know. There were a couple of sisters I probably could have wife, but I did them wrong. To be fair, sisters bring a lot of baggage to a relationship and that's mainly because of us.

Us!

We dogged them out so much. You see it in videos and our music. Plus they dogged each other out. Then the white man just wants to get in their pants that's why there always on guard.

You right, they do catch it from all angles.

John comes down the steps after ease-dropping for a few minutes on their conversation.

What are y'all smoking?

Yo, you scared the shit out of me, said Dave.

I've been up here for the last ten minutes listening to y'all bullshit. White bitches know we got that Mandingo shit. They know to treat us like kings. Sisters got that shit confused. They think their pussy is made of platinum and we are supposed to worship their ass. Fuck that!

John has spoken, said James.

Dave! How come we didn't know about this white chick?

I tryed to keep that shit on the lo'. There's a lot of shit y'all don't know. How your ass get in here away?

Your bitch-ass brother let me in. What's wrong with him anyway?

Pussy got him all fucked up. It's that first-shot syndrome. His ass is still giving her money.

Do you want me to beat some sense into him?

They all laugh, knowing they were acting the same way after there first time.

So what's up for tonight?

Let's hit Lou's. I feel like drinking and shooting some pool.

Let's go!

Lou's Place is a bar located in the center of the city. It's the spot where African-Americans go because it's neutral. You can meet chicks there who live uptown or in the bottoms.

At Lou's Place the fellas are enjoying themselves drinking and playing pool.

That's another, bragged Dave, hitting the eight ball in the corner pocket, beating John in pool for the third straight time.

Fuck you, giving him the finger.

Hey James, you play'em. I'm tired of whipping his ass. I have to go to the bathroom to let this beer out.

Five minutes after exiting the bathroom he noticed Dana.

There's Dana, all hung up on some fool. Shit, she saw me and here she comes.

Hey Dave, what'cha doing here?

Relaxing, what about you?

Enjoying myself!

I can see that.

Oh him, he's just a friend. How's your brother?

He pauses, wondering if he should answer.

He's out on a date.

Right, knowing that he's lying.

You haven't called him, he's not just gonna sit around.

Good for him, she said, playing along. You talk to Mamie? Playing the same game.

Knowing her game is as good as his, he changes the subject. Why don't you drop that brother over there and let's head back to my spot?

I thought you'd never ask.

I'll meet you outside in a few minutes.

He heads over to James and John.

Hey, I'm out!

Already? Responded James.

I have to take care of something.

Where is she? Yelled John.

Dave raises his middle finger in the air, even though he know he's right.

After a quiet ride back to the house knowing what they're planning to do, they enter through the back door.

You sure your brother's not here?

Stop worrying and bring that ass over here.

You want this ass?

I want to find out what has my brother trippin'.

You'll regret it.

Or maybe you will.

Twenty minutes later, deep into a heavy fuck session, they don't hear the basement door open and Eric walk down the steps.

Hey Dave, Moms want you to turn the music. . .

Stopping dead in his tracks, he slowly tries to focus on the face of the naked woman bouncin' up and down on top of his brother.

Dana?

Eric, she shouted.

I thought you said he wasn't here.

I don't believe you. I'm upstairs waiting on your call and you're down here fucking my brother.

Eric, I'm sorry baby, he came on to me.

Right!

She walked over to him with the blanket covering her.

I didn't mean for this to happen. Let's go to your room and talk about it.

Talk, talk, talk about what? There's nothing to talk about. I'm slow but I'm not stupid. How could you do this to me. I loved you.

I'm sorry baby, it was his fault, she beg, trying to plead her case.

I think you'd better leave.

Dave throws her clothes in her face. You heard what he said.

You set me up. Fuck you! Fuck the both of you. I got other niggas. I don't need your silly ass. I was playing you the whole time anyway, with your weak ass shot.

She puts her clothes on and leaves.

Don't worry about her, she's just saying all that shit cause she's mad. I'm sorry bro', but you wouldn't listen. This was the only way. I was tired of her hurting you.

Her hurting me, huh? You hurt me more then she ever did. Fuck her and you.

He turns and heads upstairs.

Eric, Eric? Damn, that didn't turn out the way I planned.

TRYING TO HANDLE MORE THAN ONE PARTNER

1. Make sure they work different shifts, so you can juggle the time you spend with each one.

2. Make sure they don't live in the same neighborhood.

3. Keep phone conversations short, you don't want to get in the habit of talking for hours and everyday.

4. Make sure only one has a car, so you can dictate when you spend time with the other.

5. Never park in front of your house, so they'll never know when you're home.

6. Turn cell phones off when you're in their presence.

7. Only give one your home number.

8. Make sure you meet all family members and friends so you know where not to go and who your dealing with on the street.

9. Keep her away from your family and friends, they might throw salt in your game.

10. Always change your routine.

CHAPTER 8
Friends And Enemies

Laying down in his bed in deep thought Dave receives unexcepted phone call.

Hello!.

Dave!

Who this?

Shereen.

Yeah?

Look, I'm sorry how I been treating you, I can explain everything. Just be over here tomorrow around eight.

I might be busy.

Please, I promise you, you won't regret it.

We'll see!

You just don't know what I've been through. Please be here tomorrow. Bye.

Mum huh!

He sits in silence wondering if he should go.

I wonder what's up. I shouldn't go, but you know I will.

The next day he arrives at her apartment to find out what's going on.

I'm glad you're here, she said, giving him a hug. Come on in and have a seat.

He walks in and takes a seat on the couch.

So what's up, he asked.

You don't waste any time.

All I know is that I've been thinking about you and wanting to see you and you're nowhere to be found or don't have the time.

I know! I'm sorry! Would you like something to drink?

Yes!

She goes in the kitchen and returns with his glass.

Here you go!

Red wine!

Setting up the evening.

So what happened?

All right, let me explain everything.

It takes her at least thirty minutes to explain everything that happen.

So his punk ass hopped in his car and left her while his wife and her sister beat her down.

That's some drama for you. So where is she now?

Still in the hospital, but she's feeling much better.

Look, I'm sorry! I didn't know.

Don't be! Like you said, you didn't know. So are you ready?

For what?

Dinner silly!

Like you said before. "I don't turn down a free meal".

While Dave and Shereen are busy making up, Pam has just gotten some news she wasn't expecting.

So what's the results? Asked Kelly, looking concerned.

Positive!

So are you gonna tell him?

This has to be wrong. I haven't slept with Dave in weeks.

But you don't know how many weeks you are. Who else have you been with?

Girl, you know I don't get down like that.

Kelly lowers her head.

What was that?

What?

That look, like you want to say something.

She sits there in silence wondering if she should tell her.

There's something you want to say? What? What?

Remember that day you woke up feeling kind of funny.

Yeah, it was like I was violated. I was real fucked up from drinking that forty. I went to bed naked and you know I don't do that.

Do you remember that John brought you home?

I remember him walking me to the door, but that's it. What are you getting at?

When I arrived home he was leaving our apartment and I found you in bed naked.

You what? Why didn't you wake me?

I tried!

That doesn't mean anything happened, right?

There's something I never told you.

What?

Back when you and John were real tight, he came over to see you one day but you weren't home. So he stayed awhile and we talked. Everything was fine until out of the blue he jumped on top of me and started tearing my clothes off.

What?

He was too strong to fight, so I stopped struggling. He relaxed, and as he was raping me I slid my hand over and managed to grab the lamp and bust him in the head. Then I ran into the bedroom and locked the door and told him I was gonna call the cops. He left once he heard that.

Oh Kellly! I'm so sorry. You could have told me. I'm sorry you had to walk around with that burden.

I felt ashamed! Plus y'all were real close. I didn't know if you would believe me, as tears roll down her face.

I can't believe this, said Pam massage her temples.

You okay, asked Kelly?

Not really! I'm trying to piece together what happen that night.

Where you going?

To see John!

Want me to go with you?

I got this!

Meanwhile Shereen and Dave are finishing up their food.

So how was dinner? Asked Shereen.

It was great!

So are you ready for dessert?

Sure, what you got?

Chocolate cake!

My favorite!

She comes back with a piece of cake tells him to sit back on the couch, she sits down next to him and starts feeding it to him.

I really feel like I can be myself around you, said Dave.

You have me feeling some type of way too.

He grabs the fork and feeds her a piece.

Do you forgive me? Giving him a peck on the lips.

It depends!

On what?

What would get me more kisses?

There's no wrong answer.

Well if that's the case. They start kissing and caressing. She takes off his shirt and starts licking his chest, then she reaches down and unbuttons his pants.

Suddenly he pulls her hand back.

What's wrong? Why did you stop me? She asks with a puzzled look.

Tonight has been perfect. I don't want to spoil it. "I can't believe I said that", he said to himself.

You won't, unless you stop me again, kissing him on the lips.

Shereen please, pushing her hand back once more. I do want you, I really do. For some reason it doesn't feel right. There are things I want you to know about me. I want to be on the up and up with you. Until then, I think we should wait.

You don't want to talk about it now.

I'm not ready!

She stares at him wondering what's going on.

Okay, we'll wait then! This is so hard to believe. A man turning down sex. I knew there was something special about you.

You're the special one. That's why I want to wait.

They settle with just laying in each other arms all night.

Meanwhile Pam is at John's residents about to question him about what happened that night.

What are you doing here? Said John.

I'm here to see you.

Do you want to come in?

No! I just need you to answer a few questions.

What?

Remember that night when you walked me home?

Yeah!

What happened?

You don't remember? I walked you home and you invited me upstairs to talk, because you were upset with Dave.

Then what?

We both were drinking. One thing lead to another, and you know.

Know what?

We started getting it on.

What? I would never sleep with you.

You did that night.

I don't believe you!

Hey, that's what happened and it was good. You were doing things I didn't know you had in you.

She slapped him across the face.

Don't get mad at me, laughing at her.

She tries to calm herself down, before continuing.

What about Kelly?

What about her?

Did you rape her?

What? Girl please! You'd better get out of here with that bullshit. I'm going back in the house.

I don't remember what happened that night, And I'm glad I don't remember because I sure is was a nightmare, you rapist.

See ya!

Oh yeah, another thing. I'm pregnant!

What?

You heard me.

You'd better talk to Dave.

Oh trust me, I will!

He slams the door in her face.

It's been days, and Eric still hasn't spoken to his brother.

Hey E? Hey E? Don't tell me you're still mad. I was trying to show you the light.

That's what you call it, answered Eric.

She ain't worth us.

Right! I guess you didn't think about that.

That's all I could think of at the time.

You didn't want her?

No, he responded with a little hesitation.

Like I figure! What do you want anyway?

I have a lady friend coming over for dinner and I want you to meet her.

Isn't that going against the player's code?

So what, she's special!

Eric gives he a bewilder look.

You're in love, he asked.

Slow down with that, just be here!

I might be busy.

Just try then, knowing that he's lying.

Later that evening as expected the doorbell rings and Dave goes to answer it.

I got it! He yelled as he opens the door. What are you doing here?

You aren't happy to see me? Smile Pamela.

I thought you didn't want to be bothered.

We need to talk.

You caught me at a bad time.

What I have to say won't take long.

And that is?

She gets straight to the point. I'm pregnant.

What? As he falls back against the door trying to maintain his balance. We always use condoms.

No we didn't and you know it.

Shit! How many weeks?

Don't know yet.

He stands there speechless.

So what do you want to do?

I'm keeping it.

I can't believe this! Look, we're having some company coming over. I can't handle this right now. I'll call you later.

I thought you would be happy; you don't love me.

Look, I'll talk to you later, okay? This is a lot to handle.

You'd better call me, Oh yeah, don't think I forgot about that other chick, she said before walking away.

I can't believe, I fucked up!

Staring up at the night sky thinking about what she just told him, he doesn't even notice Shereen walk up.

You miss me that much that you waited outside for me.

Hey baby, he responded snapping out of his trance and giving her a hug and kiss. You scared the shit out of me.

You okay?

No, I got some news I wasn't ready for.

Want to talk about it? She asked.

Not right now! I just want to enjoy the evening with you.

Where's Mom? I want to meet her.

I'm sorry, come on in!

As they enjoying a evening of dinner, Shereen and Dave's Mom take the time to get acquainted.

You're the first young lady friend of his he has invited to dinner. So why are you so special? Asked Dave's mother.

I don't know. Dave! They both turn and look at him?

Mom, come on!

I just want to know about the woman who has my baby on cloud nine.

Eric finally returns home.

Boy? Their mother shouted. Why are you just getting here?

I had to work late, looking at Dave out the corner of his eye.

Grab a plate and sit down to eat.

Shereen! This is my little brother Eric. Eric, Shereen!

Hi, said Eric!

Hello Eric! So who is lucky to have who?

I guess me! He really knows how to look out for me, right Dave?

Dave ignores his comment.

After dinner Dave and Shereen decided to go back to her apartment.

Dinner was great. I really like your mom. She was funny.

Yeah, I can tell she likes you too.

Do you want to come in?

I'm sorry. I have to get up early.

I understand, sounding disappointed. Well, you be careful going home.

He gives her a kiss on the lips and leaves.

A few minutes pass by and there is a knock at the door. Wondering if Dave has changed his mind, she rushes to open it.

What, you changed your mind? She said, while opening the door, I thought you were in jail.

They didn't arrest me, bitch, said Wayne, slapping her across the face and knocking her to the ground. But they arrested my wife and her sisters.

What do you want? She shouted, crawling on the floor, trying to get away.

To give you back the hell you caused me. Kicking her in the stomach.

Stop, please stop! She yelled with tears streaming down her cheeks.

Fuck that! He kicks her again and then proceeds tearing off her clothes.

No, she hollered, crying and trying to get to her feet. All of a sudden there's another knock on the door.

Quiet, bitch!

Shereen, Shereen! It's Dave. I changed my mind.

He knows I'm here.

Get up! Get rid of him.

She cracks the door.

Hey, I'm tired now! I'll talk to you tomorrow.

Girl, stop playing, pushing his way in.

Dave, look out, she yelled.

Wayne swings at him but misses. Dave pushes him to the ground and jumps on him. They toss and turn, throwing punches. Wayne is getting the best of him.

Take that, you punk-ass bitch, said Wayne, kicking him.

He looks around the room and sees a wooden bat in the corner and rushes to grab it.

Your ass is dead now, said Wayne, standing over Dave holding the bat above his head ready to swing.

Pow, pow, pow.

What the? Hollered Dave, covering up on the floor.

He slowly raises his head and standing there holding a smoking gun is Shereen. While Wayne body lays on the floor in his own blood with three shots to the chest.

Oh my God, she uttered, standing there motionless, not believing what she just done.

Um, Shereen, um I'm gonna take that please. He grabs the gun from her trembling hands. What are you doing with this?

I can't believe I just did that, dropping down to her knees, crying with her face in her hands.

Everything will be okay. I'm here with you! If it wasn't for you, I could be dead right now.

I know! But what are we gonna do? I never killed anyone.

When the police get here, we will just tell them the truth.

She thinks she did it more for Lisa then for Dave.

MAIN GIRL VS SIDE CHICK

1. Main Girl, you wine and dine; Side Chick, gets fast food.

2. Main Girl, you can say "I love you"; don't cross that line with the Side Chick.

3. Main Girl, you slowly bring out the freak; Side Chick, you go all out, with protection of course.

4. Main Girl, you show your soft side; Side Chick, you keep your feelings in check.

5. Main Girl, you can show off; Side Chick, keep it discreet.

6. Main Girl, you can shower with gifts; Side Chick, gets nothing.

7. Main Gir,l five-star hotel; Side Chick, cheap motel.

8. Main Girl, can know private things about you; Side Chick, shouldn't know more than your first name.

9. Main Girl, give you problems, work it out; Side Chick, you just replace.

10. Main Girl, you keep yo niggaz in check; Side Chick, ain't worth dying over.

CHAPTER 9
Consequences

It's been a week and Dave has been making numerous attempts to try and talk to Shereen, but she keep making excuses.

Hey baby, how you feel?

Hey, I really don't feel like talking right now, she answered.

You want me to come over?

No, that's okay!

You've been avoiding me since the incident. You didn't go through it by yourself.

I just need time to be alone right now to collect my thoughts.

You shouldn't be alone.

But I want to.

I'm coming by!

I won't answer the door.

Fine! If that's the way you want it, he yelled hanging up on her.

I'm kind of glad she said no. I've been feeling sick all week.

His phone rings and he quickly answers it, thinking it's Shereen calling him back.

Hello Shereen, picking up the phone.

No, this ain't no fucking Shereen.

Pam, oh, what do you want?

I want to know what we are going do about this fucking baby?

Shit if I know!

What happen to you bringing your ass over here? It's been a week.

I'll think about it! I'm feeling real fucked up right now, throwing up and feeling light headed.

See! A real woman would be over there taking care of you.

I don't need this right now.

Forget you, slamming the phone in his ear.

Shit, what am I going to do? First I need to see a damn doctor.

After hanging up on Dave, Pam rushes over to answer her door.

Oh, you have some nerve.

Can I come in? Asked John.

For what! So you can rape me again.

Can you let me explain?

Explain what? You're a crazy psycho.

I love you.

That ain't love it's madness.

Can you hear me out?

Hear you out! Fuck you! Fuck Dave! I might be walking around with a baby growing inside of me because your ass probably drug me. Know what?

What?

I'm telling Dave and the cops, she bluffed to get him to leave.

For what? There's nothing to tell.

I'm calling! She walks over and picks up the phone.

No, quickly grabbing her.

Get off me!

He snatches the phone out her hand and they start tussling.

I can't let you!

He slides his hands up around her neck and he starts squeezing.

I can't let you!

No, please, trying to catch her breath.

His grip overpowers her and holds on until her body falls limp.

Driving down the street to see Pamela, realizing he can't avoid her any longer, Dave notice someone who looks familiar.

Is that John leaving Pam's place? Not to concern he doesn't give it a second thought.

He then proceeds to parks his car and walks up to the door to get buzzed in.

Ringing her buzzer numerous times, he gets no response.

I can't believe she's not here. Where the hell did she go that quick? Fuck all these bitches!

Spending time at the mall to clear his mind, Eric runs into Jenny.

Hey Eric, over here, shouted Jenny standing in front of a clothing store.

Hey Jenny! This is where you work?

Yes, I told you before. Why haven't you called me or stopped by?

I have a lot on my mind.

You look troubled. I'm about to clock out. Why don't we go get something to eat?

I'm not really hungry.

Well I am! Give me a minute and you can tell me what's up.

While Jenny is eating her food, Eric is explaining everything that took place between Dave and Dana.

Look, what your brother did was wrong, but I think in his own way he probably did it because he loves you.

I can't believe you're taking his side.

I'm not taking his side. Look, how long have we been friends?

Since middle school!

We always had a special friendship.

Yeah!

Well, there's something I never told you.

This doesn't sound good!

Back during our early high school days, when I use to come over a lot. I develop a liken to your brother.

So you were using me!

Sort of! I had a big crush on him. One day, I came by your house but you weren't home. Your brother answered the door in a towel, body dripping wet.

Why are you telling me this?

Anyway! I tried to seduce him, and know what he said?

Spread em'!

No stupid! He said that you sit up every night talking about me and how you like me.

He told you!

Yeah! And that he didn't want to hurt you and that I seemed like a sweet girl.

He said all that!

I felt real stupid. He said he wasn't gonna tell you and that I should wake up cause you are real special.

He said I was special!

Yes, and he was right: You are special. That's why I been coming at you so strong since then, but you never caught on.

So you really want to be with me.

Yes! Giving him a kiss on the lips.

So it's all about you and me.

You and me, but it's up to you.

The next day at the Doctor's office.

I glad he was able to schedule me in on short notice, said Dave to himself.

I hope Denise isn't working today. I really don't want to hear no drama, as he opens the door to the doctor office.

Shit, she's here! Looking right at her seated behind the receptionist desk. He looks around the room and notice he's the only patient here.

It's been years since I been here. I see things haven't change. Looking around the room at the pictures of famous African Americans like Charles Drew hanging on the clean white walls over the brown cushion single chairs that line the room on top of the plush green carpet.

Good morning Mr. Alright, said Denise with a smile showing her sparkling white teeth.

Why do you always do that?

Do what?

Call me Mr. Alright!

Because I'm at work, so I have to be professional Mr. Scared of commitment.

You won't let that go. I told you when we first got together, don't expect nothing. Your stuff was the bomb, but not enough for a young brother like me to want a relationship.

That's what wrong with young brothers.

What!

Y'all want your cake and eat it too.

Hey! If I don't have to beg for a slice, I'm gonna eat that and the whole damn cake. Plus you love the way I eat.

She blushes and lowers her head to hide her reaction.

I'm kind of fiendin' for some right now.

Give me your five dollar co-pay and sit yo ass down. A nurse will let you know when the doctor is ready to see you. You better call me tonight too.

I will!

He sits in the chair and notice Denise peeking up at him while she does her work.

Maybe in the future I could see myself with her. She's a pretty light-skinned young girl, kind of looks like Vanessa Williams in her playboy days. Those green eyes are so hypnotizing and her long brown hair, I remember grabbing a fist full of that from the back. Plus she's tall and slim, easy to pick up and maneuver into so many positions. She should have been a model. All that and she's not a stuck up bitch.

I would have never talk to her that day on the elevator when I was coming in for a physical if I knew she was the new receptionist. I don't like being put in a situation where I have to see you if things don't work out, plus she has access to all my information.

But she was looking fine in that pink scrub she was wearing, I couldn't let her get away.

He starts reminiscing about the day they first met.

How u doing? My name is David, and yours?

Denise!

If they had you modeling that scrub your wearing in a magazine, every guy would buy his women one.

She responds to his comment with a little chuckle and thank you.

Your very pretty.

Thank you once again! I'm okay!

Girl, your crazy! A guy would wife you on looks alone.

Would you, as her eyes widen with anticipation?

I would have to get to know your inner beauty.

That's good, cause I'm more then just a pretty face.

I'm sure you are. If I gave you my number, would you give me a call so I can find out.

You have a pen and paper.

Yeah! I'll right it down...Here you go.

Make sure you call me so we can go out.

I'll think about it, fifth floor, my stop.

Me too! Where you headed?

I'm starting my new job as a receptionist for a Dr. Johnson.

Really! That's my Doctor.

How is he?

He's a middle age white guy, short, kind of losing his hair, nerdy looking glasses, he looks like George from Seinfeld, plus he likes to crack corny jokes. I just laugh to make him feel good, but he knows his stuff, keeps me healthy. Here we are, opening the door for her, good luck.

Thank you!

I'll talk to you before I leave.

Okay!

When we talked on the phone the conversation went pretty smooth, so we decided to hook up one Saturday night.

Saturday night comes around and I pick her up at her apartment. I remember when she opened the door my mouth wanted to drop, but I played it cool even thou she look amazing. She was wearing a tight black dress that came to her inner thigh and it sparkle all over. I think I said " You look very pretty".

Thank you!

Are you ready?

Yes!

I let her walk in front of me, so I can see her walk. You can tell a lot about a women by the way she walks. Like if she has confidence in herself and if her pussy is good. She definely had "I'm the shit walk".

I was being a perfect gentlemen, opening doors, giving her compliments every ten minutes, making her smile and laugh. I made reservations for us to eat dinner at Warmdaddy's, a nice soul-food restaurant located on Delaware Ave. The hostess seated us in the corner, which I preferred so I wouldn't be notice by anyone you never know who's watching. The lights were dim, a single lighted candle place in the middle of the table. We drink wine while we talked. I let her do all of the talking asking her questions, making it seem like I was interested in her life, plus I don't like telling my business. I just glaze into her eyes while she went on about whatever, I really wasn't paying attention, I just made it seem like it by saying, "Really and uh huh" after each break in the conversation.

Finally are food came, we order the same thing, baby back ribs smother in bbq-sauce which were nice and tender, yams were sweet and the mac and cheese melted in your mouth. After dinner we jetted over to south street to the Laff house to check out the comedy show.

Sommore with her double dds was perfroming, just my luck she was talking about sex and men who know how to blow a chick back out, which I think turn her on.

After the show, just to make sure the night ended the way I wanted. I took her to the art museum. We park around back in the make out spot, their were plenty of cars park back there with there windows steam. I put on Gerald Levert "Get Your Groove On" cd , then put my lips into action, giving her little pecks on her soft shiny lips which tasted like cherry lip gloss, then her neck as my right hand worked its way up between her thighs. What do you know, no panties! So I give my fingers a work out, making her cream all over my hand. Before you know it were back at her place and I got her bent over the arm rest of her blue sofa screaming her ass off. Of course I jetted when we were finish so I couldn't even describe anything in there but her couch. "You would think she knew the deal".

Nope!

She kept calling me everyday after that four or five times a day until she talked to me. She wanted me to come over all the time, plus spend the night. You know I did a couple of times because the shit was good. After three months of this, which is pass my limit with being with a chick, she asked me to move in. I was tempted since I live at home with my parents, but I know that's an relationship move, which want against the rules. I told her I'll think about it and just went cold turkey. No call backs. She never knew where I live, so I was cool. Until I ran into her four months later in the mall. But she didn't trip! She blame herself for being to aggressive. She said she miss me and still has feelings. I lied and told her I got back with my ex, (pick one).

And that was it!

A nurse walks into the waiting room, snapping him of his thoughts.

Mr. Alright the doctor is ready to see you.

Twenty minutes later The doctor walks back in after examining Dave.

So what's wrong with me? He asked.

It could be a few things. I'm going give you a prescription to get filled out and we'll take things farther once the results come back on the blood work we took. It should be back in a couple of days. I'll give you a call, so take it easy.

All right Doc! Whatever you say. Don't have me waiting too long.

After leaving the Doctor's office Dave went home to rest but is quickly awaken by a phone call.

Hello! Hey you. . . Just getting home from the doctor's office, I'm not feeling too well. . . . Oh, you can make me feel better. Your around the corner.............What you doing around there?............................. Yeah! You can come by.

Later that evening, the doorbell rings while Dave's mother is cleaning up and she answers it.

Hey Missy, haven't seen you in awhile. Dave's downstairs. He's not feeling well.

After greeting his mother she heads downstairs.

What the—?

Shereen! Dave shouted.

Who's she? She shouted.

The chick turns around and jumps off him.

Oh, I remember you. You're the bitch from the restaurant, the one you said don't worry about.

Shereen listen!

To what? How it just happened? I'm sitting at home feeling bad about how I've been treating you and you're fucking this bitch.

Bitch! Who you calling a bitch?

Girl, don't go there. I already killed one muthafucker.

Yeah, she did!

Know what? Have fun, I'm out.

Shereen, Shereen, he shouted, running after her.

Boy, get downstairs and put some clothes on, his mom shouted.

Don't worry about that bitch, said the waitress.

What! I think your ass better leave.

It's like that?

Yeah, it's like that!

Well take me home then.

He reached on his dresser and grabs a few dollar bills and throws it her at. Take the bus or call a cab.

Depressed about what happen with Shereen, wondering what he's going do. Dave just been moping around for the last three days.

Boy, how long you going lay around? Asked his mother, staring at him lying on the couch.

I messed up big time, plus I don't feel well, coughing and covering his mouth.

Yeah, you did!

So what do I do?

What, no answers? I thought you were the man.

Mom!

Don't Mom me! See where that player stuff got you. Treating women like a piece of meat. It will always come back to hurt you. You think I don't know what goes on around here. You're just like your father.

Like Dad!

Your Dad used to spread himself around! When I found out, I told him, them or me.

And?

I'm glad he found the Lord before he past.

Did you trust'em?

I trust God! I seen something in his eyes when he made that choice.

So you're saying I need to grow up and take my ass over there.

Yes and do some serious begging. . . . Well, get moving!

Right!

Hold on! Your sweating, you coming down with a fever.

I told you I been feeling real bad.

You take anything?

Everyday! I already went to the doc.

What he say?

Don't know yet, he gave me some pills.

As Dave is about to get up he's interrupted by a call on his cordless phone.

Maybe that's her!

Hello? Kelly? What'cha you want, he asked with an attitude?

You need to come over here.

For what?

Can you just come over.

After the way you treated me.

Pam's dead!

She's what? What happened?

Can you just come over?

I'm on my way!

What's wrong? Asked his mother, looking concerned.

A friend of mine is dead. I have to go.

After getting to Pam's apartment like lightning, Kelly tells him what happened.

Murdered! He falls down in a chair. They find the killer?

No!

I'm surprised I haven't been questioned as he tries to hold back his tears.

I never told them about you.

How come?

I know you're a cheater, but I also know you wouldn't do anything like this.

She tell you she was pregnant?

Yeah, she told me! We were going to discuss what to do.

You, her, and John!

John! Why John?

She didn't tell you?

Tell me what?

She hesitates, wondering if she should tell him.

This is not the time to hold back. Spill it!

She starts running down everything about what John did to her and Pam.

He did what? Naw, that's my nigga! He couldn't have!

He's your boy and all, but he can't be trusted.

We go way back. Then he recalls the day he thought he saw John leaving here. When was she murdered?

Last week!

Why you wait til now to call me.

I don't know!

I have to go. Will talk once I find something out. He couldn't have.

I told the police about your boy.

Look, I'll talk to you later.

Knowing where to find John, Dave heads to Lou's.

What, you finally found time for your boys, said James.

What's up James, John? Replied Dave.

What's up nigga? John answered. Keeping his eyes focus on his beer sitting on the bar counter.

We need to talk, said Dave, looking at John.

About what?

Let's go outside and discuss it.

I ain't yo bitch! Whatever you have to say, say it.

You sure you want to do this here?

What nigga?

Did you rape Pam?

What?

Why the fuck do you care?

So you did.

Did I say I did?

You didn't say you didn't.

You treated her like shit.

Maybe, but I would never have physically hurt her.

Fuck you!

I sure you know she's dead!

What? Said James, trying to figure out what's going on.

That's fucked up! John answered.

She was murdered!

Who did it? Asked James.

That's what I'm trying to find out.

What you tryin' to say? Said John, getting defensive.

You tell me! I saw you leave her place the day she was supposedly murdered.

John turns and looks at him, then at James. Let's go outside. Stay here James!

They go outside to the parking lot to talk, located on the side of the building. There are only a few cars in it and a couple of whinos slouch up against the wall.

Did you kill her?

Do you think I killed her?

Answer the fuckin' question!

Fuck her and you!

What?

Fed up with the games, Dave punches him in the face and knocks him to the ground. John picks up a bottle lying next to him and busted Dave in the head, knocking him down and leaving a small cut on his forehead.

Fuck you, spited John, running away.

When Dave got home he sees Eric in the living room sitting on the couch.

Damn, what happen to you? Asked Eric.

A fight!

Looks like you lost.

I don't need your fuckin' jokes right now.

I wasn't joking. You want me to get Mom?

Naw, grab me some ice, a glass of water, and a couple of tylenol. I'll be downstairs.

He sits on his bed, with his head in his lap, trying to collect his thoughts.

I don't believe that nigga.

Here you go bro, coming back giving him the bag of ice.

Thanks man!

What happen?

I don't want to talk about it right now.

You gonna be all right?

Yeah, good looking out!

Of course! You would do the same for me, smiling at him and letting him know everything is cool between them before he goes back upstairs.

Sorry, I snapped on you.

It's cool, were cool! Holla if you need me. He heads back upstairs.

My head is killing me.

He looks over at the answering machine and noticed the light blinking.

I have a message.

He pushes the button.

Bleep!

This is Dr. Johnson. Your results came in and I scheduled you to come in tomorrow. It's urgent!

He sounds serious. Guess I gotta go see him tomorrow, he lays down and falls asleep.

CHAPTER 10
The Truth

Dave sits anxiously in the doctor's office, wondering what's going on. The doctor finally enters.

How are you feeling, Mr. Alright?

You tell me!

Well, it's like this, like I said your results came back.

And?

How can I put this?

What?

You tested positive for the H.I.V. virus.

I'm what?

You're H.I.V. positive.

I can't believe this! You mean I've been walking around here all this time while my body is slowly deteriorating. But how?

There are numerous ways.

Like what? I'm not a fag.

Unprotected sex is one major factor.

This has to be mistake.

How many sex partners have you had?

I guess one too many.

How about drug use?

Never!

Blood transfusion?

I hate needles.

There are some other questions I need you to answer.

Doc, if you don't mind, I have to go. This is too much right now.

I understand, but we need to discuss the necessary steps you need to take.

For what? He walks out.

On his way out he looks at Denise, you better get yourself check out and he exits.

At home in the basement, lying down in his bed, in deep thought Dave is trying to figure out how he's gonna handle his situation.

I can't believe this shit finally caught up with me. H.I.V. positive, never in a million years would I had thought I would catch it. I tried to be careful. I know I slip up a few times, but none of the women I slept with look sick as far as I can remember. Who am I kidding you can't tell if someone has H.I.V., unless there real sick. I don't even know how many women I slept with. Now what do I do. Do I call them all and ask, do I tell them I have it. I don't even think I have any of there numbers. I just gave'em mine and when they call I was there to give them some loving. Fucking H.I.V. I bet you it was a chick fucking with a down low brotha, acting all hard like he's a thug but taken it up the ass behind close doors. Or it was someone fucking with a nigga who probably spent time in jail and his ass got took. Or a bitch was probably a straight ho, fucking and sucking with no protection. I wish dad was here. I still remember back in the day hanging out with him, watching him work his magic on the ladies. He used to lie to me and say they were friends, but I knew what was up. That's why I know what to say and how to get these women to do what I want. Women know were full of shit, but as long as we tell them what they want to hear, they don't care. What the fuck am I gonna do. Pam's dead. So there won't be no Dave Jr. And Shereen, Shereen, I finally met someone I'm actually in love with and I fuck up every chance of being with her. I'm glad we never slept together. I don't know what to do. Then the fellas, I know James is gonna be hurt. Fuck John! And Eric, idolizes me like I'm invincible. How do I tell him his big brother is dying. I have to think about what I'm gonna do. I don't like people taking care of me or have to depend on somebody. Fuck that!

Suddenly James comes downstairs breaking his train of thought.
What's up?
You don't want to know. Damn! What happen to your face?
I ran into Killer Mike and his crew. After you and John went outside, Let me tell you what happen, a couple of guys step to me. I was like "What's up".
One of them said "Come with me".
I said "For what".

He said "Somebody wants to talk to you".

I said "Well they better bring their ass to me".

So one of them grab my arm and said "Let's go". So I punch him in his face. Then the other one sucker punch me, which knock me off balance. Then out of nowhere this big six-six muther-fucker hit me and that's all she wrote. I woke up in the back of Lou's where you can lounge, on one of the couches with Killer Mike and ten other niggas drinking and smoking around me.

He let you live.

Yeah! He believe me when I told him I didn't know she was a young girl.

I repeat, he let you live.

Yeah man! He said he knows she's spoiled.

I told him I ended it, but she said she would make up some lie, to get me killed.

Killer Mike, started laughing. She played you, gee. I don't want to kill you. You may not know this, but I know who you are. I had my people do a background check.

I was like "You did".

He said "Yeah". Your Uncle is KC.

I said "Is that a good thing or a bad thing.

He said "It's a good thing. We use to do business before I got sent up. I gave him a call the other day to discuss some business, which included you. So we work some things out. He cut me a deal so his favorite nephew can live.

I open my mouth and said "Why? Doesn't he has more street credentials".

He gave me a evil look. "For now. But he owes me. He should have been in the same jail cell with me, but that's another story".

I asked "Can I go".

He said "You can go".

You're a lucky muther-fucker, said Dave.

Tell me about it. Remind me to thank my uncle. I heard what happened when you and John went outside, you don't look to good.

Yeah, I know, coughing.

That's why I'm here.

Fuck him. I have other problems.

Hear me out. John came over my house the next morning and told me everything.

I really don't want to hear this.

Let me finish. I didn't know he was that fucked up in the head.

Come on! You know his dad was a womanizer and a wife beater. Why you think his mom left. I just don't know why see left him in that type of environment.

I guess "Like father, like son" But anyway, he wants to see you so he can apologize.

What! He's a murderer. What can he say? Plus he knows where I live.

I know, but he can't come here.

I really don't care, but why not?

He turned himself into the police.

He what?

He came to my house, and told me everything, he asked me to walk him to the police station to turn himself in. He couldn't deal with the guilt. He really loved that girl and it hurt him bad when she dissed him for you. So grab your shit and let's go.

I can't!

Come on! We have too much history not to talk things out.

I can't! Yanking his arm back. There's something I need to tell you.

Tell me on the way there.

He takes a deep breath and spills it, "I'm H.I.V. positive.

What? Quickly letting his hand go and slowly sitting on the bed. You serious?

Yeah.

That's fucked up, shaking his head.

I know.

When did you find out?

I just came from the Doc.

Are you sure?

They ran the test twice.

Maybe they mixed your test up with someone else.

No mix up. That's why I been feeling real shitty lately.

Damn! I thought you were Superman.

I ran into some kryptonite.

Who gave it to you?

Come on man. I slept with so many women, who knows. So shit doesn't matter now; my life is over.

You gonna give up like that.

I'm already dead.

Come on man. It's plenty of people living with it, normal lives at that. You have H.I.V. not A.I.D.S.

They both the same as far as I'm concern.

What about your mom and brother?

What about them?

They need you.

I can't do anything for them anymore. I just want to be alone, if you don't mind.

I can't leave you like this.

What can you do. Just go tell John he did the right thing and why I can't come.

I'm sure he'll understand.

You know I'm here for you. He walks over and embraces him.

Eric comes downstairs as James is walking up the steps.

What's up James?

Hey E, passing him with his head down.

What's wrong with him, he looks like he just lost his best friend.

Yo, I need to talk to you, said Dave.

About what? I told you everything is cool, especially since Jenny.

You really like her.

I always liked her.

Yeah, I know, she's cool.

Thanks to you. I'm gonna always listen to you.

That's cool. But you have to weed out the bullshit from the real shit, you understand.

Yeah, I got you. Is that what you wanted to tell me?

He hesitated, yeah man, that's it. Go see your girl.

A few days passed, and Shereen walks in her apartment after working out.

Let's see what came in the mail. Sorting through her mail, she finds a letter with no return address.

Dear Shereen,

I'm sorry for hurting you. There's no excuse for what I done. I never thought I would fall in love, especially so quickly. I never knew what love was until the day you walked out of my life and how much it hurt. I was always the type to never let my guard down. I don't expect you to forgive me, but I'm grateful for the time you spent in my life. You made me realize what it takes to be a man. Too bad it's too late. I just recently found out that I'm H.I.V. positive....

She lets the letter slip through her fingers and it falls to the floor.

After waiting a few seconds trying to get the courage to continue, she picks it back up

Even though we never slept together, I think you should get yourself checked out. Once again, I'm sorry. I pray to God that you're not infected. I don't know if I'm gonna be able to handle this. So if you don't hear from me again, remember that I love you.

Dave

What does he mean? Oh my God. She grabs her keys and quickly exits out the front door.

Walking in his room after coming back from the store, Eric sees a letter on his bed, picks it up, and begins reading it.

Hey Bro,

I just want you to know how proud I am of you, to see you grow from a boy to a man. I know you always looked up to me, but to be honest, I always looked up to you. Stay the way you are, and don't let anyone change you. Stay focused and treat women the way you want moms to be treated. The reason for this letter is I went to the doctors last week and found out that I'm....

The doorbell rings, interrupting him.

Eric, get the door, yelled his mom.

He runs down the stairs to open the door holding the letter in his hand.

Where's your brother? Said Shereen in a panic.

I guess he's downstairs. What's wrong?

She pushes him aside and runs downstairs.

What did he do now? He says to himself as he continues reading the letter.........

....found out that I'm H.I.V. positive.

What, no, no, it can't be.

He starts heading toward basement while reading the letter.

I don't want to be a burden to moms and you or have people feeling sorry for me. . . .

He continues on while walking down the steps.

Don't make the same mistakes I made. Just one time can be fatal. I love you.

Bro! Bro!

He sees Shereen crying and holding Dave's head as his lifeless body lays in her arms, with an empty container of sleeping pills in his hand.

Please no. Please, he whispered, walking over to him.

Wake up. C'mon, wake up. Shaking his body.

He sits on the edge of the bed.

Believe it or not, you taught me a lot. I love you. He grabs his hand and kisses him on the forehead.

THE END

About the author......

Equise Smith grew up in the northeast section of Philadelphia, Pennsylvania. He now resides in Delaware County. He currently works for an transportation company as a railroad mechanic. He enjoys writing in his spare time. A graduated of Franklin Learning Center High School, he is working on furthering his education in communication. *Player's Anthem* is his first published book. If you have any questions or comments about the book you can log onto myspace. com/equisejacquel

www.ingramcontent.com/pod-product-compliance
Lightning Source LLC
Chambersburg PA
CBHW020246290526
45784CB00003B/1112